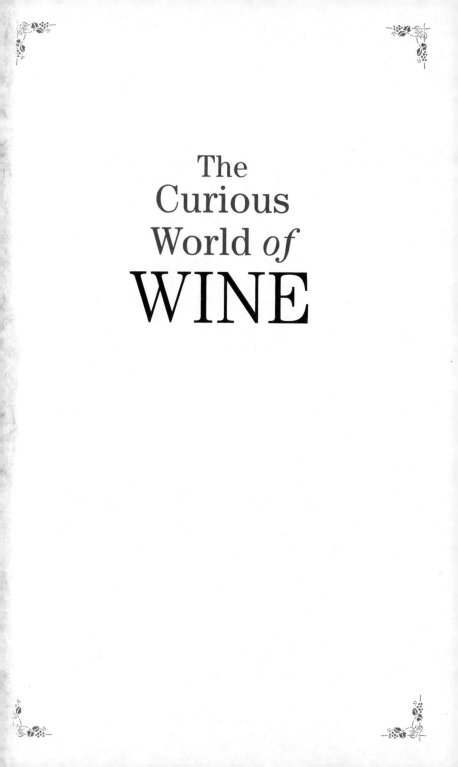

The
Curious
World *of*
WINE

The Curious World of WINE

FACTS, LEGENDS, AND
LORE ABOUT THE DRINK
WE LOVE SO MUCH

Richard Vine, PhD

A Perigee Book

A PERIGEE BOOK
Published by the Penguin Group
Penguin Group (USA) Inc.
375 Hudson Street, New York, New York 10014, USA

Penguin Group (Canada), 90 Eglinton Avenue East, Suite 700, Toronto, Ontario M4P 2Y3, Canada (a
division of Pearson Penguin Canada Inc.) • Penguin Books Ltd., 80 Strand, London WC2R 0RL,
England • Penguin Group Ireland, 25 St. Stephen's Green, Dublin 2, Ireland (a division of Penguin
Books Ltd.) • Penguin Group (Australia), 250 Camberwell Road, Camberwell, Victoria 3124, Australia
(a division of Pearson Australia Group Pty. Ltd.) • Penguin Books India Pvt. Ltd., 11 Community
Centre, Panchsheel Park, New Delhi—110 017, India • Penguin Group (NZ), 67 Apollo Drive,
Rosedale, Auckland 0632, New Zealand (a division of Pearson New Zealand Ltd.) • Penguin Books
(South Africa) (Pty.) Ltd., 24 Sturdee Avenue, Rosebank, Johannesburg 2196, South Africa
Penguin Books Ltd., Registered Offices: 80 Strand, London WC2R 0RL, England

While the author has made every effort to provide accurate telephone numbers, Internet addresses,
and other contact information at the time of publication, neither the publisher nor the author
assumes any responsibility for errors, or for changes that occur after publication. Further, the
publisher does not have any control over and does not assume any responsibility for author or third-
party websites or their content.

First edition: November 2012

Library of Congress Cataloging-in-Publication Data

Vine, Richard.
The curious world of wine : facts, legends, and lore about the drink we
love so much / Richard Vine, PhD.
pages   cm
"A Perigee book."
Includes bibliographical references.
ISBN 978-0-399-53763-9 (hardback)
1. Wine and wine making. 2. Wine—Folklore. I. Title.
TP548.V482   2012
663'.2—dc23   2012024528

PRINTED IN THE UNITED STATES OF AMERICA

10 9 8 7 6 5 4 3 2 1

Most Perigee books are available at special quantity discounts for bulk purchases for sales
promotions, premiums, fund-raising, or educational use. Special books, or book excerpts,
can also be created to fit specific needs. For details, write: Special Markets, Penguin Group
(USA) Inc., 375 Hudson Street, New York, New York 10014.

To My Family
Gaye, a loving wife for more than 50 years,
and
our three great children,
Scott Cameron
Sabrina Marie
Stacia Nicole

CONTENTS

THE THOUGHT OF meeting the person responsible for the supply of wines to American Airlines was rather daunting. We were to consider purchases of several thousand bottles and a corresponding number of dollars. I envisaged a somewhat overpowering sort of character, who would try to squeeze the last chance of profit from us, the hopeful suppliers, and whose appreciation of wine might be of secondary importance.

I met instead Dr. Richard Vine, professor of enology emeritus, a gentle, friendly man whose knowledge of wine was far superior to my own. Whilst defending the interests of American Airlines, he seemed to accept that a fair deal for both

sides was a sensible way to do business. And this we did for many years, most of which included an enjoyable and instructive lunch at our chateau, usually with the additional, thoroughly appreciated presence of his wife, Gaye.

Upon Richard's retirement, these happy occasions sadly came to an end but left us with happy memories of Dr. and Mrs. Vine.

In the meantime, he has written a book titled *The Curious World of Wine*, which will for sure bring great pleasure to wine enthusiasts across the world.

Not to be missed.

—ANTHONY BARTON
SEVENTEENTH-GENERATION
BORDEAUX ESTATE PROPRIETOR
CHÂTEAU LEOVILLE-BARTON
CHÂTEAU LANGOA-BARTON

INTRODUCTION

PROFESSOR ROBERT SMILEY, who directs wine business programs at the University of California at Davis, once remarked, "Wine is a product that most of us know very little about that we buy a lot."

At first I questioned this statement. We enjoy a full range of modern media that provide wine reviews, tasting scores, and competition medals—all giving us valuable knowledge for our buying decisions. Each new vintage results in yet another round of critique fodder for the wine scribes. We are also blessed with how-to books, websites, and media programs offering various inventive notions for wine storage, wine service, wine travel, wine cookery, wine and food matching, and even wine auctions. But do all of these still leave us without the knowledge that Dr. Smiley suggests?

For some wine lovers, each bottle satisfies by simply pouring out drinking pleasure: passionate color, seductive aroma, vivid flavor, delicately balanced structure, and good value for money. Fair enough, but for enthusiasts who integrate wine into a lifestyle beyond just a nice match with dinner, perhaps there is more. Sharing some alluring wine stories might make dining a bit more interesting and maybe even a bit tastier too.

This book tells about some of the colorful characters, celebrated places, and quirky events that make such wine stories a fascinating topic. Some of the tales are amusing, others are a tad serious, and still others, a bit naughty. For example, would most sparkling wine devotees believe that a famous Champagne vintner was arrested as a Confederate spy during the American Civil War? Does hearing that one of the most prestigious California wineries was conceived in the bedroom of a French chateau stir up some racy notions? Without much thought, we commonly raise and touch our wineglasses in a toast, wishing each other health, or as the French say, *Santé!* But why? And why do we call this ritual a *toast*? Such simple bits of wine knowledge can enrich our lives and those of our friends too.

Who has not at one time or another wanted to offer a few entertaining wine tales to rescue a gathering from some boring, self-impressed wine snob? My vision was to put together a small selection of some lesser-known wine stories, told in a light and engaging tone, that I hoped everyone could enjoy—not just wine buffs. With a career in wine spanning five decades and dozens of both national and international wine travels, I have filed away plenty of delightful fables and facts. Research to confirm them led to even more charming stories that needed to be shared.

This book should be a fun read while helping you get to know a little more about what we buy a lot.

—RICHARD P. VINE, PhD

1

Wining with the Ancients

WINE IS PROBABLY the third oldest beverage—after mother's milk and, of course, water. Beer lovers may disagree, but that's a case for them to make.

Imagine cave dwellers drinking the pulpy juice frothing from some grapes that had been crushed in a stone bowl a day or two earlier. Perhaps it was cave women who made such tipples while their suitors stalked unwary prey for dinner.

The "magic" of fermentation continued from Stone Age times until the early nineteenth century, when science took over. Frenchman Joseph Louis Gay-Lussac figured out that sugars were transformed into ethyl alcohol, carbon dioxide gas, and some heat energy. But what made this happen? That question remained a mystery until several decades later, when another Frenchman, Louis Pasteur, first saw under his microscope some one-celled plants called "yeast" that had taken harbor on the outside of a sample of grape berry skins.

There is considerably greater sugar content in grapes than in grains, and thus ancient wines had more alcohol than did ancient beers. From that extra boost of alcohol we can perceive a major historical reality: wine was a

3

better medicine, a better digestive, and a better love potion than other drinks. It was also the quickest buzz—at least up until, rather ironically, the prohibitionist Moors discovered distillation in the Middle Ages.

Anyone who truly enjoys wine has probably at one time or another fantasized about being able to hang out with the ancients and share some of their favorite vintages. This chapter looks in on some wine moments from much earlier times.

––––⌘––––

STONE AGE WINE

The best clues for Stone Age winemaking are from archaeological digs that found packs of grape seeds along the lakeshores of southern Europe. It's easy to think that these caches were left from grapes that had been

made into wine. In a few days, a stew of froth, skins, and seeds was transformed into the ancient idea of wine. Such quill probably wasn't representative of *la dolce vita*, but it was likely one of the most festive things Stone Age people had. It quenched parched palates and likely helped relieve systems straining to digest what one must think were some truly unsavory foraged meats. An essential bonus was that a little alcohol relieved the drinkers' aches and pains.

NOAH AND MOUNT ARARAT

As a descendant of Adam and Eve, Methuselah was truly ancient. There are no indications that he was either a winemaker or a wine drinker, but his grandson Noah was. Most everyone knows the biblical saga of Noah's ark drifting on floodwaters and finally coming to rest on Mount Ararat, after which he planted vines, made

wine, and got drunk. It didn't happen quite that quickly, of course, because it takes at least a couple of years for young vines to bear fruit. The question is begged as to what Noah may have drunk while waiting for his first vintage.

Ararat rises upward of thirteen thousand feet. Surely the flood level never reached that high, and the famous ark more likely came to settle on the lower slopes, where weather conditions were more conducive to Noah's winegrowing. At the foot of Ararat are the headwaters of the Tigris and Euphrates river basin—a fertile plain aptly named the Ararat Valley. Could this have been where, or near where, Noah's vine's were planted? Whether or not, many experts agree that this area is the site of the earliest winegrowing. Any doubts about the veracity of this theory were diminished by the 2010 discovery of the ruins of an ancient winery near a small town in nearby Armenia. Dated at more than six thousand years old, it is the earliest winery ever. Archaeologists also found the world's oldest shoe at the same site—perhaps removed just before its owner jumped into the grape-stomping pit?

—❦—

The oldest known vine variety still cultivated is Rkatsiteli, which was thought to be grown five thousand years ago by Georgians, just north of modern Armenia in Asia Minor.

—❦—

HAMMURABI'S BABYLON

Babylon, the "Gate of Gods," emerged during the twenty-third century BCE about fifty miles south of present-day Baghdad in Iraq.

It grew to become a prominent city—both in size and in the development of a powerful militaristic culture that brought wine into everyday consumption.

Hollywood adventure films have created some sensuous scenes for us: bejeweled palace lords gluttonously filling themselves with the richest foods and wines while being fanned by scantily clad maidens.

Only the privileged Babylonians drank wine, and most of it was imported. The Greek historian Herodotus described small bowl-shaped boats made of willow frames covered with animal skins and lined with straw that secured wooden casks of wine as they were shipped downriver from Armenia to Babylon. After the wine was sold, the men would break up their boats to sell the straw and willow branches; then they'd load up the animal skins on donkeys and trek back to Armenia. Perhaps this was a way to get out of town quickly after having sold some bad wine. Hammurabi ruled from 1795 to 1750 BCE, and one of his laws threatened the loss of a hand or some other valuable body part for any merchant selling bad wine as good. Unfortunately, good wine could easily turn bad because there were no effective long-term preservatives at the time. It's a curious notion to think that some wine dealers might have innocently lost a limb because of bacteria that nobody could see.

———◦◦◦———

NEBUCHADNEZZAR'S BABYLON

The city of Babylon was the center of ancient Mesopotamia, a region that used the oil seeping from the ground as a valuable treatment for bleeding cuts and aching muscles. Agriculture was well established, and farmers produced bounties of fruits and vegetables along with barley, rye, sorghum, and wheat for both baking and brewing. Intense summer heat did not favor vine culture, but local date wine was made. It wasn't popular then and isn't today either, but

that's an academic issue because wine is now prohibited in the region by Islamic rule. On the other hand, nowadays a blind eye is turned to wine brought in for private consumption.

Circa 575 BCE, Babylonians were under King Nebuchadnezzar's rule. He had come away from a raid on Jerusalem twenty-two years earlier with treasure in both precious riches and skilled Hebrew craftsmen, both of which were needed for building the legendary Hanging Gardens.

Nebuchadnezzar had several heavily guarded palaces. When he drank wine, it was in a secluded setting and was served by Hebrew slaves. While sipping, the king was entertained by a lusty harem protected by eunuchs, perhaps in much the fashion depicted in the tales of *The Thousand and One Nights*.

The white wine of Babylon's aristocrats might have included something similar to those made from Rkatsiteli or Voskehat grapes grown in the Ararat Valley today. Reds could be from varieties much like contemporary Areni or Kakhet grapes. One especially fragrant and expensive wine was Chalybonium, grown in Helbon vineyards near Damascus in Syria.

THE HANDWRITING ON THE WALL

Nebuchadnezzar was succeeded by five kings in just eight years; Belshazzar was the fifth, ascending to rule in 553 BCE. Such instability exemplified Babylon's rapid decline. The Bible tells of a scene in which the patricians and harlots at Belshazzar's feast drank wine from sacred gold and silver goblets that Nebuchadnezzar had pillaged from Jerusalem. It's a story found in the Old Testament's Book of Daniel, which denounces the feast as a lewd celebration. As the account unfolds, a hand is seen writing the following phrase on the wall: *mene mene tekel upharsin*. Controversy arose over the meaning, but Daniel, a Hebrew scholar, deciphered it as "Thou art weighed in the balance and art found wanting." The hard-partying Babylonians ignored the judgment and continued to guzzle from the stolen goblets, even as their kingdom was in free fall. The final verse recounts Belshazzar being slain that very same night. Indeed, he had not seen "the handwriting on the wall," an expression that yet today remains a warning for ignoring impending peril.

THE EGYPTIAN GIFT FROM GOD

There is a good chance that Egypt's first vines may have been brought from Armenia, some nine hundred

miles to the northeast. Whether or not, the Egyptians took to wine with unbridled enthusiasm. Indeed, it was decreed a gift from Osiris, their most divine god, portrayed in ancient hieroglyphics as "Lord of the vine in flower." Treatment for skin cuts was a styptic made of wine infused with Memphis stone powder. Those suffering from urinary dysfunction or in need of an effective laxative were often prescribed wine infused with various herbs. Queen Nefertiti, wife of Pharaoh Akhenaten and mother of Tutankhamun, used perfumes made with wine. Depression was treated with a styptic of wine mixed with opium. Pain was, of course, eased with sufficient wine just by itself. Vines and wines were such an essential part of ancient Egyptian life and culture that pharaohs were buried in their great pyramids with grape seeds, a promise of wine forever in the hereafter.

❧ Back from the Hereafter ❧

MUCH, PERHAPS most, of ancient Egyptian wine was red, and there were some mystical ideas attached to drinking it. Among these was that wine's red color was due to the blood reincarnated from those who had been in conflict with the gods. Another notion was that the high euphoria experienced from excessive drinking was thought to be an ancestral reprisal. As might be expected, neither of these celestial motivations seemed to dissuade red wine revelers.

PHARAOH'S WINE

Circa 2580 BCE, Pharaoh Khufu was building the first great pyramid at Giza for his hereafter tomb, paying his several hundred thousand workers with rations of bread, vegetables, and beer. Wine made from dates, pomegranates, and palm tree sap was common, but it was grape wines that the nobles coveted—and most of the vineyards and wineries were owned by Khufu and other royals, along with other members of the privileged aristocracy. Wines typically had some level of sweetness due to incomplete fermentation, the addition of honey, or both.

Popular Egyptian-grown quaffs included Taeniotic, which was said to have been fragrant and a bit astringent; Shedeh, a pricey red; and perhaps an Arp Hut grown from vines cultivated near

the city of Anthylla in southern Egypt. Popular sweet whites were Mareotic and Taeniotic along with Sebennys, a bargain blend.

Whatever wine was poured, it was usually drunk from decorative shallow bowls. Tasters would sample the wine before serving. There were questions of purity, quality, and, most important, safety from those who would wreak poison on the powerful ruler. Once it was clear that the taster would survive, Khufu would take a drink and then might satisfy his fascination for magic by calling in some illusionists for entertainment.

TUTANKHAMUN'S TABLE

Dining with King Tut would have surely been elaborate. Folks bathed and anointed themselves with oils and scents—a welcomed social gesture during hot Egyptian days circa 1330 BCE. The selection of fruits, vegetables, grains, fish, and fowl would have been rather traditional and based on agricultural products and game that Egyptians had been eating for centuries. On the other hand, cooking techniques and the use of seasonings, such as cumin, coriander, dill, and mustard, were evolving and supplemented the more common oils and vinegars. Even if underage drinking had been an issue then, Tut would have been exempt: He was

◈ *Heavenly Wine* ◈

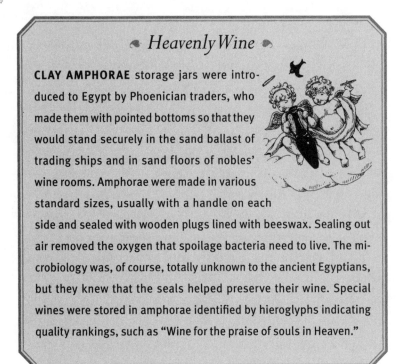

CLAY AMPHORAE storage jars were introduced to Egypt by Phoenician traders, who made them with pointed bottoms so that they would stand securely in the sand ballast of trading ships and in sand floors of nobles' wine rooms. Amphorae were made in various standard sizes, usually with a handle on each side and sealed with wooden plugs lined with beeswax. Sealing out air removed the oxygen that spoilage bacteria need to live. The microbiology was, of course, totally unknown to the ancient Egyptians, but they knew that the seals helped preserve their wine. Special wines were stored in amphorae identified by hieroglyphs indicating quality rankings, such as "Wine for the praise of souls in Heaven."

the king and had his own stash of wine. Selections were made from amphorae, often identified by hieroglyphic tags providing detailed information relating to vintage and vintner. Table service included alabaster, bronze, silver, and gold, complete with finger bowls. Appetites might have been stimulated by dinnertime entertainment. Belly dancing, an erotic art form, had wiggled its way from Babylon to Egypt more than a hundred years earlier.

ISRAEL'S BIBLICAL WINE

The fifth book of the Old Testament is Deuteronomy, a book some consider to be the words of Moses, and that includes the Ten

Commandments handed down to him from God. Deuteronomy also contains some social laws, such as the one found in verse 23:24:

When thou comest into thy neighbour's vineyard, then thou mayest eat grapes thy fill at thine own pleasure; but thou shalt not put any in thy vessel.

Such was the welcoming character found in the foothills of Judea, where baskets of grapes were taken to stone basins and trodden, and the juice was collected and fermented in pottery jars. Archaeological digs at Gibeon just a few miles north of Jerusalem have found several dozen handles from wine jars inscribed with the names of local

⬥ *Land of Milk and Honey* ⬥

JOSHUA AND Caleb were two young followers of Moses who were sent to Palestine as spies to confirm that the Promised Land was truly the land of milk and honey. The two emissaries returned carrying a huge cluster of grapes—so large, in fact, it was carried on a pole between them. While fruit of such dimension is difficult to imagine and is likely exaggeration, the Aramon variety regularly yields clusters that can reach up to seven pounds each. Winemaking existed in grand proportions; archaeological investigations have unearthed a large number of vats that served entire communities. The popular Canaan wine of Palestine was sweetened with honey and infused with spices. It was quaffed by Hebrews at meals and dutifully blessed for ceremonies—apparently tasty stuff because it was also an export to Egypt.

vintners. The Arab conquest in 636 CE, four years after the death of Mohammed, ended winegrowing in Israel for more than a thousand years.

SOCRATES AND HIPPOCRATES

The Hellenic, or Golden Age, of Greece circa 510–323 BCE diminished barbarism and fostered human rights. Democratic government was an idea born in Greece, as were the disciplines of economics, education, and mathematics as well as the arts of literature, theater, and architecture. Any concerns today about how we govern, earn, learn, and create can be directed to the original precepts of Greek thinkers twenty-five hundred years ago.

Ancient Greeks, like Egyptians, not only enjoyed wine but depended on it for more than a simple beverage. It replaced foul water.

Socrates related the role of wine to his students in Xenophon's fifth-century BCE *Symposium*:

So far as drinking is concerned,
gentlemen, you have my approval.
Wine moistens the soul and lulls
our grief to sleep while it also
wakens kindly feelings.

Hippocrates, "the Father of
Modern Medicine" and
whose famous oath is still
sworn by graduating
physicians, used wine as
the base for his impressive
list of medications.

New World winemakers are
today often called *enologists* from
the Greek *oinos* (wine) and *logos*
(logic). British English takes the
purer spelling *oenologists*.

GREEK SYMPOSIA: GOLDEN AGE TASTINGS

Perhaps the first educational
classroom was the *andron*—a
special place where men could
hold a *symposium*, which translates
as "drinking together." These
Golden Age gatherings were
typically devoted more toward
enjoying food, wine, dancing
nymphs, and enticing music than
academic presentations, but
nonetheless, the men
attending them discussed
various topics. A typical
symposium would comprise
a group of up to two
dozen or so participants
hosted by a *symposiarch*,
who directed the program
and brought some measure of
balance between pleasure and
purpose.

After everyone had eaten,
there were tributes made with
three different wines: one to the
lesser gods, one to the ancestors,
and one to the supreme god,
Zeus. It was considered heathen
to drink wine, whether at a
symposium or in private or
public, without first mixing it
with seawater unpolluted by
urban sewage; the alcohol helped
sanitize the water and perhaps
soften the wine's acidity, making a
more pleasant libation.

◆ Wine Fiasco ◆

THE ANCIENT Greek custom for diluting wine was to add the water by mixing it in a large wide-mouth jar called a *krater*, which was shared among those present. A plain drinking cup was called a *skyphos*. Special occasions might call for a vessel made from an animal horn, called a *rhyton*, which was typically decorated with the donor beast's head carved at the pointed end.

Wines were sometimes stored in a *lagynos*, a type of earthen-ware container protected by a wicker-like exterior that may have been a prelude to the wicker-covered Italian *fiasco* bottles familiar to ordinary Chianti wines from Tuscany. Given today's labor and material costs, there are few wines bottled in wicker fiascoes. It is curious, though, that Chianti may have once been so bad that the word *fiasco* is now often used for something gone wildly awry.

DIONYSUS ENTERS THE SCENE

Hollywood has portrayed ancient orgies as wickedly ribald festivals of group sex. In the real world of the ancients, these love-ins were sometimes rites of passion that could become deadly. Dionysus was the Greek god of wine and life; we can understand a god of wine, but why a god of life as well? Anyone with an invitation to one of his orgies had to be exceedingly careful; a few cups of wine generally led to chanting and dancing, festivities that typically grew increasingly louder and sexually suggestive as part of the rites of worshiping Dionysus. This phase commenced an embrace of the god's spiritual presence, which

often descended from pleasure to cruelty and even bloodshed, making for some gripping plots in ancient Greek theater.

A TASTE FOR RETSINA

Greeks were the first civilization in which commoners regularly drank wine—much of it an amber-white wine called Retsina. As the name suggests, it was infused with tree resins, which served as a preservative but also gave off a rather noxious turpentine-like odor. Everyday drinking was from the *phiale*, a stylized footed drinking cup; today's Greeks prefer tumbler-like glasses for their Retsina. This is one of the few wines that offer us a taste of times two thousand years ago.

Quickly, bring me a beaker of wine so that I may whet my mind and say something clever.

—Aristophanes, Greek playwright, *Knights* (fourth century BCE)

THE EMPIRE RISES UP

Among the eighth- and seventh-century BCE Greek colonies in Italy preceding the emergence of the Roman Empire was Enotria Tellus (Land of Wine). This particular settlement was in what is now known as the Calabria region, where vines of Greek heritage are still cultivated and carry names such as Greco Bianco (Greek white) and Greco Nero (Greek red).

Wine was also made in Etruscan settlements across what is now Tuscany, long before the great empire was created. One of the most favored red wines by the Roman founding fathers was made from Sangiovese vines, a name taken from the Latin *Sanguis Jovis* (blood of Jupiter), high praise because Jupiter (Zeus in Greece) was the god of gods.

Early Roman society had some very savage laws. Among them was the curious forbiddance of women to drink wine. A husband catching his wife taking a nip was free to divorce her or even take her life. If he didn't kill her, perhaps the wine would, because much of it was preserved by storing or serving it in lead containers, which also enhanced flavor and sweetness.

The oldest glass wine bottle found to date is a fourth-century Roman amphora-shaped flagon discovered near the town of Speyer, Germany, in 1867.

WINE AT THE FORUM

Winegrowers in Cumae, a fourth-century BCE Greek colony near Mount Vesuvius, made a dense red wine that the poet Martial called "immortal Falernum"—so dark and rich that it aged for decades. Falernum, also known as Falernian, was among the favorite wines of Julius Caesar, along with imports from the Greek islands of Chios and Lesbos.

The southern foot of the Italian geographical boot was emerging as a respected winegrowing region. The wines of Abruzzi, mainly Consentia, Rhegium, and Tempsa, were ordinary; those of Calabria, principally Babia, Galea, Status, Trebellicum, and Veliternus, were generally considered superior by most wine aficionados, along with Surrentinum, which often required several decades of aging before drinking. Emperor Caligula, who had a thirst for strong red wine, rejected Calabrian offerings, calling them *nobilis vappa* (noble plonk).

Imperial Rome was the capital of the empire and the capital of wine drinking, averaging more than a pint per day per person. Gladiators and slaves were given Lora, an "after-wine," which was a weak swill made by adding water to fermented grape skins out of the grape press. Soldiers drank Mulsum, an ordinary quaff sweetened with honey that was affordable by the masses and was given to the poor to elicit civil behavior and political support.

■

Wine brings to light the hidden secrets of the soul, gives being to our hope, bids the coward fight, drives dull care away, and

teaches new means for the

accomplishments of our

wishes.

—Horace, Roman philosopher and poet
(65–8 BCE)

ROMAN CONVIVIA: REVELRY WITH CLASS

Anyone curious about his place in the Roman social pecking order could try wangling an invitation to a *convivium*—perhaps loosely compared to a social businessmen's club of today. The gathering's host would serve the best food and wine to the most important citizens and provide lesser quaffs and fare to the other guests, who were often clientele invited because of their association with business and political schemes. The status of civic standing held by each individual governed the quality of wine that he was allowed to drink.

Unlike the large *kraters* that served everyone at Greek symposia, each participant in the

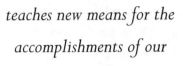

Classy Wine

THE CIVIC ranking of people was the basis of Roman paranoia, especially for lesser classes who had limited access to superior goods. In the early 160s BCE, there were statutes set forth specifying constraints on expenditures for daily food and wine, ensuring that the lowly did live low on the hog, so to speak. Other restrictions eventually evolved into building codes that required residences to have windows facing the street so authorities could monitor what was being eaten and drunk.

❧ *Erotic Emetophiliacs* ❧

EATING TO excess was common in ancient Rome, even expected, as some of the most lavish residences featured rooms that served as vomitoria. Some hosts opted to maintain slaves to carry barf bowls to those appearing ready to disgorge. Servants assigned such duty would carry a handy towel to wipe up any spittle, allowing revelers a prompt return to the table for more gluttony. In some circles, emetophilia was the popular social mode—the act of upchucking on naked bodies followed by rinsing with a golden shower—acts that somehow aroused erotic stimulation. With today's media pretty much unbridled in content, it is curious why such Roman-style dinners are not graphically portrayed for us in some modern mode.

Roman convivia had his own small personal vessel in which to mix water with his wine. Persons of lowest status were regularly exposed to the indignation of censure or jest. Convivia were generally less structured gatherings than the Greek symposia and thus perhaps a bit more fun. On the other hand, they were surely less effective in advancing education and new ideas.

Group guest rankings at some modern-day gatherings may also seem to be determined by the quality of wines poured at the free bar.

---⧓⧓⧓---

NOBLE ROMANS

Toga-attired guests arriving at a Roman senator's home for dinner would be served in his *triclinium*, a plush dining area for reclining and enjoying the service of slaves. Dishes of beans, cabbage, carrots, cucumbers, radishes, and other vegetables were routinely prepared with imported spices, olive oil, and vinegar. Fish, fowl, meat, and sausage entrees were grilled and usually presented with bread, figs, and grapes. Senior guests were partial to oyster entrees that were thought to enhance male virility—a notion that has vividly lived on in male hopefuls around the world. Pots, pans, dishes, and goblets of the gentry were often made of metals containing lead, as were chastity belts. While such hardware doubtlessly served well as the latter, it was unfortunately a very toxic dinner service.

---⧓⧓⧓---

BACCHUS: ROMAN GOD OF WINE AND REVELRY

The Romans adopted and renamed most of the ancient Greek gods. Thus Aphrodite, Greek goddess of love, became Venus; Athena, Greek goddess of wisdom, became

Minerva; Poseidon, Greek god of the sea, became Neptune; and, Dionysus, Greek god of wine and life, became Bacchus.

The Bacchanalian revelry of Rome continued much in the same manner as the rites of Dionysus had in Greece. The first Bacchanals were annual wine celebrations attended only by women. These grew to become monthly trysts and then, as might be expected, men started getting into the act. It was these that became the pagan Bacchanalian rites of gluttony and sexual debauchery that have been etched in bawdy college fraternity toga festivities ever since.

While lacking the extreme tragedy of Greek mythology, the Roman carousals nonetheless eventually became violent and often ended in bloodshed. As a result, the Roman Bacchanalia prompted suspicion as the

spawning ground of plots for crime and conspiracies against the empire, prompting the 186 BCE Roman Senate passage of the Senatus Consultum de Bacchanalibus, which banned any further public wine celebrations.

END OF THE EMPIRE: BEGINNING OF THE CHURCH

Christ was born during an age when wine drinking had become well established and was at the center of life throughout the Roman Empire. Wine was essential as a quaff with meals and vital on the battlefield as both beverage and medication. It was also the most important stock for trade, and thus growing

wine anywhere in the empire outside of Italy was forbidden. There can be little surprise in learning that such restrictions were widely ignored.

Relics of the times repeated Christ's declaration that *Ego eimi I ampelos* (I am the vine), which refers to wine as a symbol of his blood sacrifice. Red wine had, however, figured into the spiritual imagery of human blood long before the advent of Christianity. The ancient Jewish prayer the *kiddush* was a precedent and still uses wine as part of this sanctification prayer. Persians, Babylonians, Egyptians, and Greeks all had sin offerings of blood, albeit not always human blood. Some of these cultures used goat blood for religious ceremonies, from which the term *scapegoat* may have originated.

BIBLICAL WINE

Differences of opinion exist as to just what wine was in biblical writings. Some insist that references to the Hebrew *yayin* (wine) were meant as grape juice. Perhaps, but it remains curious why about two dozen of the Bible's wine citations are warnings against abuse if it simply referred to unfermented juice.

The Bible contains more than 225 references to wine, far more than for beer, called *shakar* by the ancient Hebrews. There are indications that some shakar was made from dates and fruits other than grapes. Dates and fruits make wine, of course, not beer.

Bottom line, although we may not know precisely how many times the Bible makes reference to wine, we do know that it was an essential part of life in biblical times. Consider the following verses that equate wine with merriment, health, and spirit:

JUDGES 9:27
And they went out into the fields, and gathered their vineyards, and trode the grapes, and made merry.

1 TIMOTHY 5:23
Drink no longer water, but use a little wine for thy stomach's sake and thine often infirmities.

PSALMS 104:15
And wine that maketh glad the heart of man, and oil to make his face to shine, and bread which strengtheneth man's heart.

PSALMS 23:5
Thou preparest a table before me in the presence of mine enemies: thou anointest my head with oil; my cup runneth over.

An overflowing wine cup indicated good fortune when the biblical books were being written. In modern times, the expression generally eludes to having more than enough.

Christianity served as a primary force in winegrowing, becoming an essential thread in the cultural fabric of the Old World. In the European settling of the New World, Christian beliefs curiously turned on wine as an instrument of the devil, serving as one of the foundations of national prohibition in America.

ST. BENEDICT: MIRACLE OF THE WINE CUP

Benedict was born circa 480 to parents of wealth in Nursia, now the region of Umbria in central Italy. As a young man of privilege, he led a life of decadence and promiscuity. But living amid the pagan violence of the final days of the Roman Empire he was inspired by the promise of the Christian faith. Subsequently, he met the monk Romanus Subiaco, who convinced young Benedict to live alone in a cave near Subiaco's monastery for three years to demonstrate the convictions needed for a life given to Christian service. Subiaco checked in on him regularly, and when the specified time was served, Benedict was given the call to become abbot for the fifteen monks who lived in the monastery.

Subiaco probably got more than he bargained for, and doubtless the monks too. Benedict led his flock in the strictest manner of Cenobite worship and mission, unlike other sects, such as the Anchorites and Sarabaites, who lived rather as hermit friars with questionable lifestyles. Benedict's clerics were constrained from all the temptation of physical pleasures. His rule required they work diligently in the monastery's gardens and vineyards. Senior monks were rationed a pound of bread along with two cooked meals daily. When available, apples and vegetables constituted a third meal. Younger men received less. The allocation of red wine was typically about one pint per day, although Benedict could authorize a bit more when it was warranted by intensive labor during summer weather. Wine was provided for bodily needs, not for satisfying the palate or dulling the mind.

In addition to such strenuous and stringent bodily demands, Benedict also required his monks to sing all the psalms of the Bible every week and standardized their

personal conduct per *Rules of the Master*, a twelve-thousand-word dictum that he wrote circa 530.

As might be expected, some of the monks became disillusioned with such rigid constraints. A conspiracy grew that ultimately rendered the decision to kill Benedict by poisoning his wine. As he blessed his fatal wine cup, it shattered, saving his life and giving the shocked monks a whole new appreciation for the power of God expressed by their leader.

2

French Connections

F RANCE HAS LED the Old World integration of wine into the art form that now fascinates epicures around the world. True, New World and Southern Hemisphere wines have proven to be as good and sometimes even better, but French wines still consistently get high scores from the wine scribes and command the dearest prices. That, plus high-rolling collectors seek out more vintages from the timeless classified caves, castles,

domaines, and chateaux of France than from any other country. The mere mention of France often conjures up images of gourmet food, expensive perfume, seductive *amour*, and, of course, fine wine.

This chapter visits some of the curiously colorful characters and distinguished landmarks that celebrate the rich legacy of France and the grape.

CHÂTEAU AUSONE: ROMAN SURVIVOR

There are few, if any, of today's winegrowing estates that have a greater reach into history than Château Ausone. It is situated prominently on the site of vineyards and a villa once owned by Ausonius, a fourth-century Roman poet and statesman.

The modest Château Ausone mansion was built in the relatively recent 1700s. It is a treasure situated amid the perfectly preserved medieval city of Saint-Émilion, named for Emilien, an eighth-century itinerant monk, who settled in a natural cave in the base of the rocky escarpment on which the city was built.

This quaint historic wine city overlooks the right bank of the Gironde estuary that meanders through the entire Bordeaux region and out to the Atlantic. Every visit to Bordeaux should include at least one day in Saint-Émilion to admire the classic medieval architecture and perhaps allow a vision of D'Artagnan and his Gascon musketeers clomping along the now very worn cobblestone streets.

Saint-Émilion was heavily quarried in the eighteenth century and became a prime source for limestone *doublerons* (blocks), used to construct

Château Ausone and many of the other sturdy buildings in the area and beyond. The underground caves that remained after the stone was removed became dwellings for human habitation—

and a haven for refugees during the French Revolution. Château Ausone rests on three of these old caves, which now serve to insulate its precious tiny annual production of red wine from both the heat of day and the cold of night.

RICHARD THE LIONHEART: DUKE OF AQUITAINE

At the tender age of fifteen, Richard Plantagenet became the duke of Aquitaine, granting him a vast region embracing the entire southwestern sector of France. What wine lover today can imagine a teenager reigning over all the vast Bordeaux wine lands and well beyond? He ascended the throne of England as Richard I, an English king who could not speak English. History probably better remembers him as Richard the Lionheart, leader of the twelfth-century Third Crusade,

who had a fierce bravado likened to that of a fearless lion.

Red wine grown in Bordeaux during Richard's time was a dark rose often called Clairet. Over the next several hundred years, the region's winegrowing evolved to achieve red wines more intense in color and character. The British loved this new darker, richer style, calling it Claret, as they still do. Brits developed such a thirst for it that thousands of chateaux were built, and quays in Bordeaux were reserved exclusively for loading shiploads of the wine to England. Special vessels were built to carry the heavy barrels and casks; these rugged ships could also easily tote big iron cannons and, in fact, did. These heavy-duty wine square-riggers eventually became the first ships in the great British armada.

While Richard I struck fear in the hearts of his mighty adversaries, it is ironic that he met his end not from bloody combat but from a boy seeking revenge for the death of his father and two brothers in battle. An arrow fired from a crossbow by the young lad struck Lionheart in the shoulder, and he later died from gangrene.

THE SEVENTEEN BARTONS OF BORDEAUX

There are a number of French winegrowing families with long tenures in Bordeaux. Ask most anyone there which family has been continually making wine there longer than any other, and they will tell you the Bartons. That would be correct—except that the Bartons aren't French, they are Irish!

It all started in 1722 when Thomas Barton emigrated from the Ireland mountain vale of Curraghmore to Bordeaux to found a wine-trading company. Grandson Hugh inherited what had become a successful wine business; he subsequently partnered with Daniel Guestier to found Barton & Guestier, one of the most prestigious wine-marketing houses in France.

Barton relatives provided sanctuary in Ireland during the French Revolution while the Guestiers kept on with the affairs of the business. Once the political scene stabilized in the early 1800s, the Bartons purchased Château Pontet Langlois, which was renamed Château Langoa-Barton. Later, family heirs to the Marquis de Las Cases sold a part of their neighboring Léoville-Las-Cases vineyards to the Barton family, which became Château Léoville-Barton. The two are operated as one estate, with the Langoa mansion at the center.

World War II gave cause for a sixteenth-generation Barton, Ronald, to take refuge back in Ireland, and again the Guestier family looked after things at the chateau properties as best they could, given the sacrifices of the times. After the war, Ronald returned to Bordeaux to manage the estates; he died in 1986. The estate then went to nephew Anthony Barton, who still directs Château Léoville-Barton and Château Langoa-Barton as Bordeaux wine jewels with a definite Irish character.

• Jefferson Had It Right •

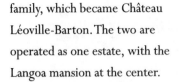

THE PARIS 1855 Classification ranked Château Léoville-Barton a Second Growth and Château Langoa-Barton a Third. This unofficial pecking order was based largely on price levels that the British market was willing to pay for the wine from each of the sixty-two grand estates in the Médoc, Graves, and Sauternes districts of Bordeaux. There were five First Growths decreed; it's curious that four of them had been proclaimed by Thomas Jefferson decades earlier as Bordeaux's best. There were fifteen Second Growths, fourteen Thirds, ten Fourths, and eighteen Fifths. Although it may seem lowly to have been called a Second or Third Growth, these designations were still exceedingly prestigious because there were several thousand chateaux wine estates in Bordeaux at the time, most of which, like both Léoville and Langoa, still exist.

BARON PHILIPPE DE ROTHSCHILD: SECOND TO NONE

Poet, sailor, actor, and auto racer, Baron Philippe de Rothschild—a member of the famous Rothschild banking family—took over operations of the prestigious 203-acre Château Mouton-Rothschild estate in 1924 at the tender age of twenty-two. The *mouton* part of the name had been ascribed to the estate well before the French Revolution. Among the French translations are "mutton" and "ram." Take your pick, but it seems likely it was originally a sheep farm.

In 1946 Baron Philippe commissioned Philippe Julian, an up-and-coming artist, to create a painting to enhance the charm of the chateau's wine label. It was highly publicized, which encouraged the baron to continue with more new masterpieces, one for each vintage. Artists included such greats as Dali, Picasso, and Warhol.

In his later years, Rothschild become rather reclusive, often conducting business in his bed chamber. Despite his ascetic lifestyle, he was very public in his scorn for the Paris 1855 Classification that had relegated his Château Mouton-Rothschild as a Second Growth instead of a

First, like the wine from neighboring Château Lafite-Rothschild, run by his cousin Baron Elie. Second Growth was a puzzling mandate because Mouton's wine fetched similar prices

to those of Lafite and the other three First Growth red wine chateaux. Rothschild embarked on a lifelong campaign with the French government to have his estate elevated to a First with an oft-publicized cry of *"Premier ne puis, Second ne daigne, Mouton suis"* (Cannot be First, won't accept Second, I am Mouton). Finally, in 1973, after decades of intense influential lobbying, Jacques Chirac, then minister of agriculture, paved what had to be a formidable French political pathway for the ascension of Château Mouton-Rothschild to First Growth status, the only change ever to have been made to the 1855 decrees.

CHÂTEAU LAFITE-ROTHSCHILD: MAGNIFICENT IRONY

Château Lafite-Rothschild is the world's most recognized fine-wine icon. If Thomas Jefferson had a list of favorite Bordeaux red wine, Lafite probably topped it. In any case, Jefferson's rapture of this grand estate did much to bring it fame and fortune.

The archaic Gascon word *lafite* refers to "top of a hill," but the earliest wine reference of the word is found in 1234, when Gombaud de Lafite, abbot of the Vertheuil Monastery, mentioned the site as a medieval fiefdom situated at or near where Lafite is today. After several lines of ownership, it was sold in 1784 to Nicolas Pierre de Pichard, the first president of the Bordeaux Parliament. This was the same year that Thomas Jefferson became American minister to France. Three years later, Jefferson visited Bordeaux and proclaimed Châteaux Lafite, Latour, Margaux, and Haut-Brion

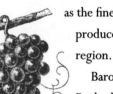

as the finest wine producers in the region.

Baron James de Rothschild, head of the renowned banking family in France, purchased Lafite in 1868, and thus the property took the Rothschild name. The baron died just a few months later, leaving the grand estate to generations of barons de Rothschild, who have maintained their old castle and classic vineyards in glorious style ever since.

Nazi air marshal Hermann Goering, well known as a patron of the arts, coveted Château Lafite-Rothschild, so much so that Hitler had planned to make it a gift to Goering. Consequently, Lafite, unlike most classic Bordeaux chateaux, was placed in the hands of the French Vichy government to protect it during the Nazi occupation. Lafite thus survived in fine fashion albeit in classic irony because after the war, the estate was returned to Baron Elie Rothschild, who was of Jewish descent.

COS D'ESTOURNEL: AN ELEPHANT IN THE CELLAR

When one travels north just past Château Lafite-Rothschild in the vaunted Médoc district of Bordeaux, the next imposing chateau seems more like a temple out of Timbuktu than one of the imposing provincial mansions typical to the region. But that is where the difference ends, as Cos d'Estournel produces equally fine red wine and arguably the finest grown in the Saint Estèphe commune.

The colorful story of this pagoda structure arises from an equally fascinating character, Louis Gaspard d'Estournel, who inherited his family's vineyard estate in 1791. He added neighboring vineyards and planted others in a quest to make fine red wines from the Cabernet and Merlot vines that were grown at

2005

GRAND CRU CLASSÉ EN 1855

COS D'ESTOURNEL

SAINT - ESTÈPHE

neighboring Château Lafite. By the time d'Estournel reached his sixties, his wines had indeed become worthy of sharing the international praise that was lauded on vintages of other regal growths in the Médoc. The red wines grown at Cos d'Estournel were the choice of kings, queens, and every manner of discriminating aristocrat.

That success brought him the means to make frequent travels to the Orient, so many that locals referred to him as a *maharaja* (great king). He became so fully enamored with the cultures in the Far East that he actually came to believe that the expense of taking his wines to India and back gave

them a special quality and provenance. Success also funded the building of a mansion in the architectural mode of Bagan, Buddhist, and other Asian styles, all topped with ornate pagodas. The arched entry bears the d'Estournel family coat of arms and has a distinct Forbidden City character, complete with a statue of an elephant in the courtyard. The charm of Château d'Estournel created an active response in the marketplace; loyal customers visited to see the very French Bordeaux wine estate that had a very Far East look.

As might be expected, Louis Gaspard d'Estournel's expensive travels and building projects landed him in financial difficulties, and he was forced to sell his wine estate in 1853. It was bad timing. Just two years later, Château d'Estournel was awarded a very prestigious Grand Cru Second Growth decree at the 1855 Paris Exposition, making the estate much more valuable for the new owner, Cecil Martyns, a London banker.

CHÂTEAU D'YQUEM: THE NOBILITY OF MOLDY GRAPES

The earliest record of the property that is now Château d'Yquem is a government document transferring ownership to Jacques de Sauvage in 1593. Two hundred years later, the marriage of Françoise Joséphine de Sauvage d'Yquem to Count Louis-Amédée de Lur-Saluces resulted in bringing the estate into the Lur-Saluces family.

Château d'Yquem fashioned a

completely different white wine from anything Thomas Jefferson had ever tasted before. In certain weather conditions, a delicate gray mold the French call *pourriture noble* (noble mold) collects on the outside of grape skins. This mold is *Botrytis cinerea*, and the microorganism has the curious facility for penetrating grape skins, allowing dehydration of the fruit, which results in concentrated sugars and flavors in the remaining juice and resulting wine. The finest Sauternes can typically improve with decades of bottle aging, achieving exceptionally long life. Château d'Yquem was the only white wine estate ranked as First Growth at the 1885 Paris Exposition.

Generations of de Sauvage and Lur-Saluces heirs faithfully maintained the domain for more than four centuries, until it became the brunt of a family feud. In 1996 controlling interest was lost to LVMH, the French marketing conglomerate that touts such mega brands as Louis Vuitton, De Beers, Dom Pérignon, and Christian Dior—the latter now offering a skin lotion made from the sap taken from Château d'Yquem vines.

CHÂTEAU CHEVAL BLANC: REGAL ON THE RIGHT BANK

Château Cheval Blanc is perhaps the epitome of red wine made from the Cabernet Franc vine. Curiously, it was not classified by the 1855 Paris Exposition, and neither were any of the grand red wine estates of the Saint-Émilion commune. It was a stroke of ignorance that heated up a long rivalry between the chateaux in the Médoc and Graves on the left bank of Bordeaux's Gironde River, and those in Saint-Émilion and Pomerol on the right bank. While Cabernet Sauvignon is the major wine variety grown on the left bank, it is Merlot and Cabernet Franc that are the principle varieties cultivated on the right, where temperatures tend to be a touch cooler during the growing season. These varieties produce, of course, different red wines, which perhaps are at the root of the contention. Also in question is nobility, both in vineyards and in vintners, as pompous displays of estate wealth are expressed on both sides of the river.

Château Cheval Blanc (White Horse Mansion) stands amid a

gravel plain a few miles west of Saint-Émilion village. It was built in 1269 by Englishman Roger Leyburn to serve coach travelers food and drink. The superior libations at the inn started a reputation that, despite any manner of order or ranking, remains among the most revered of all Bordeaux wines.

❧ *Putting Wines in Their Place* ❧

IN 1954 the Institut National des Appellations d'Origine (INAO) of France created a system for classifying Saint-Émilion viticulture, one that is actually more dynamic and has more contemporary meaning than the old static pecking order that governs their antagonists on the left bank. Each Saint-Émilion wine estate is reconsidered for status reclassification every ten years based on facilities upkeep, wine quality, market demand, price levels, and other key factors. A Saint-Émilion vineyard estate can rise up from no distinction to become a Grand Cru (Great Growth), and in turn, a Grand Cru can be voted up to a Grand Cru Classe. Those can conceivably be elevated to a Premier Grand Cru Classe—A or B. Chateaux can also be downgraded for negligence. There are only two chateaux ranked Premier Grand Cru Classe A (Cheval Blanc and Ausone), both clearly the equal of the finest red wine estates on the rival left bank.

PETRUS: PROMINENCE WITHOUT PEDIGREE

The right bank region of Pomerol has perhaps the least impressive landscape in all of Bordeaux. Plain countryside is dotted with mostly modest chateaux that pale in comparison to the grandiose mansions in the Médoc, Graves, and other left bank regions. It is thus rather curious that of the most expensive Bordeaux wines released to the marketplace, at least one from almost every vintage comes from unclassified Petrus in unranked Pomerol.

There are no class rankings of Pomerol estates. It was not included in the Paris 1855 Classification, and its vintners rejected the INAO classification system of 1954 instituted in neighboring Saint-Émilion. The Moueix family, which owns Petrus, doesn't even consider the property a chateau. Indeed, their Petrus *chai* (cellar) is a comparatively small structure that most passersby would consider perhaps a quaint up-to-date farm building, surely nothing special on the outside.

Inside, however, there is something *very* special—and also ironic. While wines from the Merlot vine are considered rather ordinary in many parts of the world, the Merlot of Petrus is a dense garnet red wine, expressing an exceptionally intense bouquet of complex cedar, black cherry, and truffle flavors. Vintages of Petrus regularly achieve perfect scores from wine critics, creating a demand for which supply has to be allocated despite new release prices that can reach rude levels. Prepare to shell out a cool $4,000 for a single bottle of the Petrus 2009 vintage.

GARAGE WINE

Millions of keen amateur winemakers around the world try

their hands (and sometimes their feet) with every vintage. For many, it is a time-honored family tradition that uses methods established generations ago. Each year the car comes out of the garage and in goes the press and some barrels for another batch of truly special wine.

It was much the same for Jean-Luc Thunevin and Murielle Andraud, who in 1989 made wine from a two-acre vineyard near the village of Saint-Émilion.

Their winery was literally their garage, dubbed Château Valandraud. The *chateau* part of the name was, of course, tongue-in-cheek. The *valandraud* part stood for Murielle's maiden name, Andraud, and her homeland, the *val* (valley) of Fongaban. Amid landmark centuries-old chateaux, some producing classic red wines from estates embracing dozens of acres, Château Valandraud was almost literally a drop in the bucket.

❧ Over the Top ❧

CURIOUSLY, SUCH minuscule production of unknown Bordeaux garage wines became rather like cult favorites for enthusiasts, who found the rich intensity worth the money. Pricing for vintages of Valandraud regularly exceed $300 per bottle. As would be expected, this success attracted other "garagistes," such as Le Pin, whose price tags have reached steroid heights: 2000 vintage bottles exceed $5,000, and the 1982 more than $8,000!

The popular wine media continue to hype the garagistes, some predicting such wines as fads destined for failure. Perhaps, but even during a sluggish world economy, their producers are living the dream.

SOLDIERS OF WINE

It was Citeaux monks who created the Clos de Vougeot abbey with vineyards of Pinot Noir, both donated and purchased, during the early 1100s. The *clos* (wall) around the property was not constructed until two hundred years later. Today, the landmark priory and chapel remain perfectly preserved, much as they were after construction was completed in 1551.

The new regime in control of France after the Revolution in 1789 seized the Clos de Vougeot, as it did all church property, later auctioning them off to private bidders. Julien-Jules Ouvrard acquired the 125-acre abbey estate in 1819, a huge property by Burgundian standards. It was then a *monopole* (monopoly) vineyard, meaning the entire plot was owned by Ouvrard. Since then, the vineyard's holdings have been subdivided over and over again. Today, there are more than eighty individual proprietors, each of whom owns and cultivates specific rows of vines within the original clos, which are all classified with the lofty Grand Cru designation.

Division of the vineyards separated them from the old stone monastery, which was sold and resold; the last buyers, in 1944, were a well-healed group called the Friends of the Château Clos de Vougeot, who wanted to preserve the property. They, in turn, gave a ninety-nine-year lease to the Chevaliers du Tastevin (Soldiers of the Wine Tasting Cup), a brotherhood of Burgundy enthusiasts from all walks of life. Every November, they gather from around the world to celebrate at Clos de Vougeot during the historic wine auction at the nearby Hotel Dieu in Beaune.

❧ French Wine Classification— Wine with Complexity ❧

IN 1935, eighty years after the Paris Classification of Bordeaux chateaux, the French government enacted the Appellation d'Origine Contrôlée (AOC). The AOC was a decree that placed requirements on "wines of controlled origin," to be regulated and enforced by the Institut National des Appellations d'Origine (INAO). Many of the dividing lines were based on historical records left by medieval monks, whose monasteries had centuries of experience learning which plots of land consistently yielded grapes that made superior wine. Top-ranked vineyards were exalted as Grand Cru (Great Growths), which typically also command top prices. In 2009, the AOC was revamped, becoming the Appellation d'Origine Protégée (AOP), which included some control over lower wine classifications, boosting their competitive advantage with global wines, which are subjected to fewer regulations and thus cost less to produce. The AOP is administered differently in each wine region; thus, Alsace, Bordeaux, Burgundy, Champagne, and so on, are regulated in regard to their individual *terroir* (combination of climate and soils), traditions, vine varieties, market demands, and other distinctions.

ROMANÉE-CONTI: EPITOME OF BURGUNDY

Of the hundreds of precious tiny vineyard plots in Burgundy's Côte d'Or (Slope of Gold), there is one that stands supreme among all the rest: the four and a half acres of Grand Cru Romanée-Conti Pinot Noir vines, grown on poor clay marl soil that nurtures the most expensive red wine grown anywhere in the world.

Those fortunate enough to have tasted a vintage of Romanée-Conti might describe it as having an intense, dense ruby hue, expressing a bold bouquet that fills the nose with incredibly complex bramble, coffee, and truffle flavors, structured on a full-bodied softness that caresses the palate with lingering aftertaste. Famous wine expert Hugh Johnson has referred to such grand Burgundy as "an iron fist in a velvet glove."

Curious Burgundy lovers can take just a few minutes' stroll from this hallowed plot of vines and find vineyards that look remarkably similar and also produce tasty Pinots. Are they as good as Romanée-Conti? Not according to well-heeled

believers eager to spend upward of $10,000 per bottle for new vintage releases—and thousands more for collector vintages!

THE MONTRACHETS: ALL IN THE FAMILY

What Romanée-Conti is to Pinot Noir wine nobility, Le Montrachet is to Chardonnay wine royalty.

The Montrachet name may have arisen from the Latin *mons racemes*, translated as "grape hill," or *mons rachicensis,* "bald hill," both names given by Romans during their occupation of the region during the third- and fourth-century heyday of the Roman Empire. Documentation of Montrachet history during that time and

✤ *Montrachet Legacy* ✤

ALL OF the five related Montrachet vineyards are now ranked as Grand Cru, the pinnacle of French wine classification. As provincial Burgundy became divided into communes, they often added the name of the most prestigious vineyard in their township to their own.

As political lines were drawn, three of the regal Montrachet vineyards ended up straddling the Chassagne and Puligny communal lines. Thus, both of these townships quickly borrowed the name Montrachet for their villages, creating Chassagne-Montrachet and Puligny-Montrachet, as they are known today.

throughout the Frankish reign that followed is sparse, with much left to legend.

One such tale is that of a young man serving as a *chevalier*

(soldier) in one of the great Crusades. He had been sent off by his father, lord of the grand medieval castle of Montrachet, who remained behind to enjoy the company of the ladies in his court. One of likely many encounters with the lovely *demoiselles* produced a child. The courtiers celebrated the arrival of the *batard* (bastard) son with a joyous *bienvenue* (welcome). The duke of Burgundy, however, was not pleased with the lord's indiscretion, especially given that the lord's elder son, the *chevalier*, had recently died in battle for the Holy Land.

Years later, the castle was destroyed, and the vineyards were divided into plots, which were named to recall the ribald saga of the castle's former lord: Montrachet, Chevalier Montrachet, Bienvenue-Batard Montrachet, and Batard Montrachet.

THE BOUCHARDS: DRY GOODS TO WET GOODS

The rigors of poor soil and harsh weather have a profound effect on many classic winegrowing regions, but perhaps none as much as in Burgundy, where vines are famous for their struggle to bear small clusters of Chardonnay and Pinot Noir grapes, packed with rich color and flavor.

Michel Bouchard was a studied winemaker in the early eighteenth century, although he devoted equal time to his fabric business.

He made frequent trips to Paris with books of cloth samples, taking along small wine deliveries to help defray travel costs. In time, the cased goods business outdid the dry goods, and the reverse sides of his sample book pages were used to take wine orders for his next trip to the city. More vineyards and wine production facilities were added, and the name Bouchard Père & Fils (father and sons) became one of the largest and most prestigious wine firms in Burgundy.

The original Bouchard Père & Fils caves remain under medieval bastion walls, some more than twenty feet thick, which once guarded the medieval city of Beaune. Bouchard's *aine* (elder son), Joseph, began selling wines as a wine *negociant* (blender-bottler-marketer) for other vintners, subsequently acquiring his own vineyards and eventually establishing the Bouchard Aine negociant house in Burgundy.

DROUHIN'S HIDDEN GOLD

King John II reigned in France until his death in 1364, leaving the crown to his eldest son, Charles V. Philip II was junior among John II's sons and was awarded a duchy that encompassed much of modern-day Burgundy, becoming the first duke of Burgundy.

Duke Philip's inheritance included an expanse of vineyards originally made by monastic plantings sponsored by Charlemagne. Philip, and all the dukes of Burgundy who followed, made a fortune in wine fermented and stored in the labyrinth of old Roman munition storage caves carved out under the streets and bastions of Beaune, the capital city of Burgundy centered in the famous Côte d'Or (Slope of Gold).

In 1880 Joseph Drouhin, just twenty-two years old, moved from the Chablis district in northern Burgundy to Beaune with a bold dream. He acquired a small negociant wine-marketing house that was situated atop some of the old duchy caves. Later he bought some of the finest vineyards of the region, which a century earlier had been seized and auctioned off as spoils of the French Revolution. Drouhin used the Roman caves to hold his large inventories of fine old vintage Burgundies, including stocks from regal Romanée-Conti.

During World War I, Drouhin was accused of collaboration with the Americans and was jailed. Thus, the family came under suspicion for working with the French Resistance during World War II. Joseph's son, Maurice, sensed that the Gestapo was watching him and knew that all the classic wines in the Drouhins' caves were vulnerable for looting. Maurice directed family efforts to hide the most valuable wine in the most remote nooks and crannies of the medieval caves. Frantically they closed them off with clever fake walls covered with mold media, and the Drouhin children gathered spiders and relocated them nearby so that their webs would make the fronts look undisturbed.

As expected, the Gestapo came after Maurice, who fled into the caves, working his way in darkness through a myriad of Roman arched tunnels leading to a secret door behind some wine racks that led up, out, and away. After searching the house, the Gestapo seemed to actually believe that Maurice was indeed on a business trip to Paris, as his wife and children had insisted. Drouhin remained in hiding until the war was over;

unfortunately, when he returned home, he found the business in dire need of renovation, but he had little money with which to revive it.

Maurice did have, however, some liquid gold, still hidden behind the fake walls covered with mold and cobwebs.

BEAUJOLAIS: THE GREAT RACE

In 1395, King Philip the Bold banned the growing of Gamay vines in Burgundy, except in the Beaujolais locale. His quest was

somewhat of an ethnic cleansing of vineyards. Pinot Noir had become the pride of upper Burgundy, while the bountiful production of Gamay grapes made jammy red wines that were good for blending but much too brash on their own for distinguished palates. The move forever relegated Beaujolais as a poor cousin to the regal vineyards of the Côte d'Or.

The bold move shut down Gamay as a blending wine, which had a severely negative impact on the Beaujolais winegrowing economy. Beaujolais vintners countered by offering wines to the bistros of nearby Lyon, which provided some immediate income for needy winegrowers; each new vintage found growers hastening to deliver young wines to bars and cafes.

It remained a regional race until British wine enthusiasts in the 1960s took up the idea of how quickly new releases of Beaujolais wines could be brought to Gamay lovers in England. That evolved into a competition that was launched by the London *Sunday Times* in 1974. The first new Beaujolais was released at midnight on the third Thursday of November that year, and the first bottle had crossed the English Channel by early afternoon the next day. Thus, the London race for Beaujolais Nouveau made headlines and has since become an annual event for other cities around the world. Today, larger Beaujolais vintners go to great lengths, even at air freight expense, to gain the buzz of their brand arriving first in major global markets.

DOM PÉRIGNON: DRINKER OF STARS

Every wine enthusiast is familiar with the olive drab shield label on every bottle of Dom Pérignon Champagne. The name comes from a Benedictine monk who in

1668 was appointed wine master at the Abbey of Hautvillers, near the small city of Épernay, in the middle of the Champagne region. In Pérignon's time, Champagne vintners made their Chardonnay and Pinot Noir grapes into table wines that competed with those same varieties cultivated farther south in Burgundy. Tax burdens were reduced for whichever region produced a superior vintage. Vying for the favor of the kings often came close to a civil war.

Some say Pérignon was blind. Whether or not this is true, he was an expert in identifying wines from specific vineyards in "blind tastings," which provide no clues to the wines' identity beforehand. After years of employing this rare talent, Pérignon was recognized as a master blender of wines by the hundreds of vineyards across the Champagne region. But his place in history was made when he became one of the first winemakers to use stoppers made from the bark of cork trees to seal wine bottles. Wooden plugs, wax stoppers, oiled fabric, and other closures eventually became obsolete. Pérignon's seals were so good that wines bottled before they had fully completed fermentation retained some of the carbon dioxide gas still building within; when uncorked, these wines burst forth with festive froth and bubbles. Although records fail to document it, the legend persists that after his first taste, Pérignon exclaimed, "I am drinking stars." Whether fable or fact, we can be sure that he was a pioneer in making classic sparkling Champagne.

The newly styled sparkling wine from Champagne became a fascination for the aristocracy in France. Some thought the bubbles were therapeutic, and others proclaimed the wine an effective aphrodisiac—an idea that has not faded. King Louis XIV, the Sun King, markedly increased the wealth of France by exporting Champagne to England, where some Brits insist that their ancestry was the first to make it sparkle. The Loire Valley also claims the invention of bubbly, as does the Languedoc in southernmost France. In any case, as more and more Champenois vintners turned to making sparkling Champagne, the serious economic and political rivalry with Burgundy toned down considerably.

My dear girl, there are some things that just aren't done, such as drinking Dom Pérignon '53 above the temperature of thirty-eight degrees Fahrenheit.

—James Bond, in *Goldfinger* (1964)

♦ *Before the Bubbles* ♦

THE CHAMPAGNE region in northeastern France sits atop pockets of very old *crayeres* (deep caves), carved out by Romans fourteen hundred years ago to store their munitions. The Romans needed a consistently dark, cool place to store white phosphorus gunpowder, which can ignite in warm sunlight at temperatures of 93°F or above. Visitors to the crypts notice the moist, chalky chamber walls, which have a soft consistency, meaning it was relatively easy for the Romans to carve out the underground spaces they needed. Today, the miles and miles of crayeres under the Champagne cities of Reims and Épernay continue to maintain a year-round natural temperature in the mid-50s, perfect for the fermentation and aging of Champagne.

MERRY WIDOWS

If we credit friar Dom Pérignon with the 1668 discovery of Champagne bubbles, we must also cite two remarkable widows for their clever development of Champagne's production and marketing.

Dom Pérignon's wine had yeast residue left in the bottles, making it cloudy and unattractive. Madame Barbe-Nicole Clicquot Ponsardin set about to clean it up. She was an exceptionally bold and gifted young woman, who was widowed in 1805. Her inheritance included the Clicquot Champagne house, along with a wool-trading company and several other family businesses—all at a time when commerce was dictated by men.

The *veuve* (widow) drilled holes in a table so that the bottles could be inverted and shaken to coax the dead yeast sediment down into the necks, a process called *remuage* (riddling). A careful but rapid removal of the cork created *degorgement*, releasing the head pressure in the bottles and expelling the yeast sediment but, unfortunately, some of the wine too. That problem was fixed by freezing the neck of the bottle

before disgorging so that a small ice plug was formed, which became a sort of projectile of solidified yeast but preserved more of the wine. A finishing touch was the addition of a *dosage* of sugar syrup to replace the volume lost by the ice plug and provide a bit of residual sweetness before a final cork was driven and tied in with a taught cord. Clicquot Ponsardin's process, the *méthod champenoise*, resulted in brilliantly clear bubbling Veuve Clicquot Ponsardin Champagne. This inventive woman continues to be remembered by Veuve Clicquot Le Grande Dame, a prestige edition of Champagne made from only exceptional vintages.

The story of Madame Louise Pommery is remarkably similar to that of Madame Clicquot Ponsardin. Both inherited Champagne houses and wool-trading companies by being widowed at a young age, although they lived about a half century apart. While Clicquot's rigorous process brought clarity to bubbling wine, it was not immediately adopted by other Champagne vintners. For years some producers continued making nonsparkling table wines in the fashion of rival Burgundy. Madame Pommery was the first to adopt the *méthod champenoise* for her entire production.

It was after the truly magnificent vintage of 1874 that she made the first *brut* (dry) Champagne, which has no residual sweetness. Ridiculed by the critics as being unbalanced with excessive tartness, the wine was nevertheless a hit in the marketplace. Madame Pommery's business grew so well that she added another twelve miles of caves, networked with some of the Roman crayeres, which were the original Pommery cellars. The Louvre museum in Paris displays a number of French art works that she either purchased or commissioned. The House of Pommery honors her memory by releasing Madame Louise Champagne, brut of course, from only prime vintages.

❧ The Beauty of Champagne ❧

DURING THE Franco-Prussian War, Bismarck's soldiers occupied both Épernay and Reims. It was an encampment that did not go well. Champagne insurgents killed Prussian soldiers, which led to retaliation, resulting in the execution of many Champenois. Madame Louise Pommery was a petite woman whose charming beauty was often persuasive in gaining clemency for the accused. It was an eloquence that also served her well after the war when promoting the business of her Pommery Champagne exports.

CHAMPAGNE CHARLIE: CONFEDERATE SPY?

Floren-Louis Heidsieck founded his Champagne house in 1785. It was inherited by his three nephews in 1828, creating the three Heidsieck Champagne vintners that continue today. Henri-Louis Heidsieck formed Heidsieck Monopole. Christian Heidsieck's widow married Henri Piper and thus Piper-Heidsieck was created. Charles Heidsieck

named his piece of the pie simply Charles Heidsieck Champagne.

Charles had a particular fascination for marketing his Champagne in America and in 1852 spent a brief period establishing an import agency in New York City. His Charles Heidsieck bubbly became fabulously successful in Yankee society, and after returning to New York several years later, he found himself a cult hero—dubbed "Champagne Charlie." But his bubbles burst in 1861 when Congress passed a law that exonerated Southern debtors. Having considerable payables on his books from thirsty New Orleans enophiles, he sailed there to collect. The city was virtually broke, and he came away with a cache of cotton in payment for one account.

An attempt to smuggle his valuable cotton out of Mobile, Alabama, ended with it being lost to Confederate authorities. The French Consulate stepped in and gave Heidsieck a diplomatic pouch containing a bogus document stating the cotton was for Confederate uniforms. With the pouch in hand he was free to return to New Orleans to find passage back to France. By the time he arrived, the city had fallen to the Union and the fake document implicated him as a spy. His imprisonment was international news, known as the "Heidsieck Incident." With a series of diplomatic exchanges,

one being a direct appeal from Napoleon III to President Abraham Lincoln, Champagne Charlie was released in November 1862 after seven months of confinement.

I like Champagne because it always tastes as though my foot's asleep.

—Art Buchwald, Pulitzer Prize–winning columnist, *New York Herald Tribune*

Charles returned to Champagne in poor physical health and even poorer financial health. Several months later, however, he learned that his New York agency was transferring some property in Colorado to him in order to make right the 1861 debts. That land was part of a small community known as Denver. The land deal jump-started a fortune that was able to restore Champagne Charlie and his business back to health and fortune. He died ten years later.

~

JEAN-CHARLES HEIDSIECK: PROHIBITION BUBBLES

Thanks to extensive marketing efforts by Madame Louise Pommery and Charles "Champagne Charlie" Heidsieck, the United States became a vital market to the major Champagne vintners. When the news of national prohibition in America broke in 1919, it was a shock to all French vintners and particularly those in Champagne. But for some

it turned out to be a good thing because it ended the high U.S. customs duty, providing, of course, the French vintners could find ways to smuggle their bubbly into the United States.

Among those eager to explore such loopholes was Jean-Charles Heidsieck, grandson of the famous Champagne Charlie. He crossed the Atlantic to investigate firsthand the opportunities to continue supplying the American thirst for French bubbly. Heidsieck discovered that the French-owned islands in the Caribbean had become major depots for illegal shipments of all manner of alcohol. Boats from

✦ Getting a Leg Up ✦

BOOTLEGGING IS often ascribed solely to Prohibition, but actually it was a method used decades before to deliver alcoholic beverages to Indian reservations, where it was illegal. The name arose from flasks that were made curve shaped to fit around a leg and down inside a high-top boot.

island ports carried Champagne cases covered in waterproof, tar-soaked fabric that allowed for offshore drops. If a U.S. Coast Guard cutter spotted a delivery speedboat, the cases could be thrown overboard in shallow coastal waters and later retrieved by night for bootleggers to distribute.

COUNT DE VOGUE: CHAMPAGNE HERO

Most every Champagne fanatic would agree that the most famous of the great Grand Cru Champagnes is Dom Pérignon, made by Moët & Chandon. It is an iconic *cuvee* (blend) created in 1936 by Count Robert Jean de Vogue, who had become president of Moët six years earlier. In 1941, during the German occupation of France, de Vogue led the formation of the Comité Interprofessionnel du Vin de Champagne (CIVC). The CIVC organized industry cartel standards for the control of production, pricing, and marketing for all the growers and sparkling wine vintners in the Champagne region.

Among the greatest of all wine thirsts in Nazi Germany was that of Field Marshal Hermann Goering. He and the Nazi High Command obviously couldn't have cared less about the rules of the CIVC. They were taken with the sudden largess of Dom Pérignon, along with all of the other great Champagnes. They placed the responsibility for ensuring the flow of prime bubbly to Berlin on Otto Klaebisch, as the Nazi *Weinführer* (wine leader). Klaebisch was director of Matteus-Muller, a wine-producing and wine-marketing firm in the Rheinland.

Klaebisch's endless demand was supplied from the twenty-odd miles of Moët & Chandon Champagne storage crayeres and caves under the streets of

Épernay. As Moët's president, Count Robert Jean de Vogue was thus a figure frequently called on to ensure some of the Weinführer's orders were met. The count was also a figure frequently monitored by the Gestapo for suspicion as an active member of the defiant French underground movement.

Their suspicion was well founded. De Vogue was indeed active—far more than the *Schutzstaffel* (SS) suspected—because he was the political head of the entire French Resistance in eastern France. When this was discovered, he and his close collaborators were arrested and sent to face a Nazi military tribunal. De Vogue was convicted and sentenced for execution. In response, the Moët & Chandon employees entered into a work strike that shut down shipments of their precious sparkling wine. To avoid the German High Command's wrath from the possibility of a Champagne drought, Weinführer Klaebisch was forced to bargain, ultimately agreeing to delay carrying out de Vogue's death sentence so the flow of Champagne to Germany would continue uninterrupted.

Count de Vogue was taken to the infamous Ziegenhain prisoner-of-war camp and worked to the point of death. There was little food and drink. Gangrene set in on one of his fingers, and without medical care, he was forced to cut it off himself with a piece of broken glass. He survived to see the Allied Forces liberate France and was returned home to Épernay, where he regained his health and continued as president of Moët & Chandon. De Vogue passed away in 1976, but his cuvee Dom Pérignon and the CIVC both

remain active epitaphs of his courage and leadership.

The smashing of a perfectly good bottle of Champagne over the bow of a ship to celebrate a maiden voyage may have roots in ancient Babylon. Back then, it was a gory event, involving blood from a sacrificed ox being spilled over the prow. Most of the early Mediterranean cultures that emerged after Babylon carried forward various forms of launching rituals. Vikings launched new longboats by pouring human sacrificial blood over the prow in a spiritual appeal for good luck in its conquests. Renaissance Christians baptized new boats by casting a silver cup filled with holy water over the bow. This became rather expensive, so the British came up with a cost-saving measure that replaced the expensive silver with bottles of Champagne.

CHÂTEAUNEUF-DU-PAPE: CREATING FRENCH POPES

In response to heavy taxes levied on the French Catholic clergy, a controversy erupted between the Vatican and King Philip IV, who is often referred to as "Philip the Fair," a moniker that refers to his blond hair and light complexion. Philip levied a 50 percent income tax on French Catholic clergy, which commenced a bitter relationship with Pope Boniface VIII, who eventually excommunicated Philip in 1296. The French king was reconciled the next year, but he remained at odds with Boniface, who died in 1301 amid rumors of being poisoned. The 1303 election of Benedict XI as pope brought to power a Vatican cleric who was well educated and pious but weak in both body and spirit.

With the death of Benedict XI in 1305, Philip the Fair and French nobles moved forcefully to create their own papacy, appointing Archbishop Bertrand de Goth of Gascony as Pope Clement V. The new Vatican seat was in Avignon, the Châteauneuf-du-Pape (New Home of the Pope), and remained so until 1376.

Only several partial walls of the grand French Vatican castle remain. They are high, overlooking the Rhone River, and set in some of the most curious vineyard topography in the world. Syrah, Grenache, Mourvèdre, Cinsault, Roussane, and other regal red wine vines thrive literally in fields of stones that serve to hold precious subsoil moisture. The *galets* (pebbles) also hold daytime heat, which is released during cool nights, hastening ripening and averting the threat of frost.

3

Legends and Lore

OLD WINE LORE makes up some of our everyday clichés. The origins of these can whet the appetite for a wealth of curious legends, some of which are also still alive and well. Consider the village of Varnhalt near Baden-Baden, Germany, where vintners still fear that an entire vintage of wine can sour to ruin if the last harvest of grapes is not delivered by oxcart. Some people insist that there can be relief from hangovers by taking another drink from the same beverage, the "hair of the dog," that created the dipsomania the evening before. Experienced imbibers generally agree that such a remedy provides little or no redemption. This chapter brings to light such stray bits of wine lore that are perhaps more bizarre than curious.

TO YOUR HEALTH!

Surviving wisdom indicates that a toast was originally a deft move to splash just a small amount of wine into each other's cup to ensure that neither was being poisoned and was thus, quite literally, a wish for health! But why do we call such sentiments a *toast*? Some historians believe it is derived from Romans soaking pieces of hard bread in wine as a social fellowship that is strikingly similar to the modern celebration of the Christian communion. Perhaps a more likely take is from the Latin *tostare*, which translates as "parched" or "thirsty."

HONEYMOON SWEETNESS

Honey was the nectar of Aphrodite, the Greek goddess of love, and remained a symbol for love centuries later. Old World newlyweds once heartily drank metheglin, a blend of mead (honey wine) and water that symbolized two becoming one, confirming the serious vows that just replaced their former single freedoms. Parents provided sufficient metheglin to last throughout the wedding reception festivities and to provision the couple for a month afterward—from one moon to the next and, hence, the honeymoon. Another version is that the first month of a marriage is always the sweetest, and thus the idea of a honey month evolved into the word *honeymoon*.

LACRYMA CHRISTI: THE TEARS OF CHRIST

The southern Italian province of Campania embraces the city of Naples, with Mount Vesuvius nearby always threatening to erupt again. The volcanic slopes of Vesuvius were planted with vineyards of Aglianico vines, first brought to the slopes by Greek traders more than two thousand years ago.

Regional lore has it that Satan was exiled out of the beautiful Campanian countryside and so stole a portion of the land and cast it into the Gulf of Naples. Locals called the event "a bit of paradise dropped by the devil." When Christ came to visit the area, so the tale continues, he looked on the scene and began to weep at the devil's work. Wherever his tears fell, vines grew, creating wines of sacred origin on the devine slopes, to be evermore known as *Lacryma Christi*. Aglianico vines still flourish among other red wine varieties cultivated by vintners in the foothill vineyards of Mount Vesuvius, and winemakers still produce the Tears of Christ.

The oldest vineyard still producing grapes is thought to be in Maribor, Slovenia, where vines up to four hundred years old remain fruitful.

DRUNK AS THE POPE

For a tippler to become "as drunk as the pope" is an expression inspired by Pope Clement VI. Born as Pierre Roger, he advanced in the Roman Catholic hierarchy to become the archbishop of Rouen before King Philip IV appointed him as the fourth among seven French pontiffs seated at Avignon, the Châteauneuf-du-Pape (New

Home of the Pope), usurped from the Vatican in Rome. Clement VI's rule of the church was from 1342 to 1353, a decade in which he spent the French Vatican treasury with abandon. His lifestyle was more like a wealthy bon vivant secular prince than that of a poor priest. He bought the entire city of Avignon so he could fully wallow in his earthly pleasures, among which were the services of a harem of young women and a stable of young boys. His lasting infamy came when he celebrated Mass while drunk and thus brought papal inebriation into a standard for intoxication.

CHARLEMAGNE: NO STAINS ON HIS REPUTATION

As the first Holy Roman emperor, Charlemagne ruled Europe more than a thousand years ago. He granted parcels of French land to the church with the proviso that

monks would build abbeys, plant vineyards, and make wine. Charlemagne especially enjoyed the red wines made from the Pinot Noir vines cultivated on his large parcel of land called Corton. It is located in a prime spot at the center of the Côte d'Or, Burgundy's most prestigious vineyard district.

Legend has it that as a younger man, he self-imposed a modest but sufficient daily ration of red wine from his Corton vineyards, which he consumed voraciously without regard to a bit of drooling. As he became older, such eager gusto left a menacing

stain in his white beard. Thus, his queen encouraged him to drink only white wine in public. Fortunately, Chardonnay vines were already grown in his Corton vineyards, providing a handy alternative.

Whether this story is fable or fact, the entire Corton vineyard plot is now divided among individual owners but they still label bottles from their Pinot Noir vines Corton. Their Chardonnay vines continue to produce the fabled white wine labeled Corton-Charlemagne. Both are Grand Cru classed.

is blessed with the legend of a flying dragon that landed there and was subsequently burned by the sun. The flaming corpse was said to have spewed blood that drained into the soil, which has ever since produced tart grapes, making a high-acid wine that warms the palate.

It is called the Brand vineyard after the German word for "burned." This old story probably figured heavily into the French government decreeing it a Grand Cru. Those skeptical of the dragon tale may attribute the sharpness of Brand grapes to the vineyard's elevated, rocky, and well-drained site—all factors contributing to grapes that are dense with high acidity, creating a little burn of tartness.

THE DRAGON VINEYARD OF ALSACE

A hilltop vineyard at the entrance to the Munster Valley near the French Alsatian village of Turkheim

THE WINE WITCH OF DASENSTEIN

A glass of Hex vom Dasenstein Spatburgunder (Pinot Noir) recalls the legend of a privileged girl from Rodeck Castle near Heidelberg, whose father denied her marriage to a peasant boy. In an act of rebellion, she ran away to become a hermit on a rocky vineyard mountainside called Dasenstein across the valley. She became known as the Hex vom Dasenstein (witch of Dasenstein), although she was a good witch, who blessed the local vineyards with fine crops of grapes.

MIRACLE WINE OF THE BERNCASTELER DOCTOR

Unlike the many doctors who own wine estates in Germany, the Berncasteler Doctor is a vineyard, not a physician. The story goes that in 1360 Herr Ritter von Hunolstein offered a bottle of wine grown from his vines in Berncastel township to his personal friend Archbishop Boemund. The prelate lay gravely ill in the ancient Roman city of Trier. Boemund was grateful for this thoughtful gesture and eagerly drank his friend's wine, assuming it to be one of his last earthly pleasures. The next day he awakened from his deathbed with vitality, gesturing to the fateful bottle and proclaiming, "This splendid 'doctor' cured me!"

Hunolstein's eight-acre vineyard in the middle of the beautifully austere Mosel River wine region has forever since been known as the Berncasteler Doctor. Those fortunate to visit the Grimm's fairy tale–like village of Berncastel can take the steep trek up the Doctorberg hillside and see this story depicted in a magnificent bronze relief on the large doors that front the cellars in which this classic wine is still made.

THE BLACK CAT CELLAR: A FATEFUL FELINE

The sleepy town of Zell nestled among steep hillside vineyards along the upper Mosel River in Germany is where avid wine enthusiasts can find the fabled Zeller Schwarze Katz (Black Cat Cellar). Zeller folks tell of a superstitious innkeeper at the Electoral Castle Inn, who, after years of scant profits from his hotel, started growing grapes to supplement his income.

It was on a cool rainy day just before his premier harvest that he suddenly came across a black cat between the vineyard rows. It was an encounter that startled both the keeper and the cat. The terrified feline humped his back, hissed, spit, and scampered away while the aspiring vintner fell into despair at the grim omen of bad luck.

But depression slowly turned to delight as his grapes began ripening to perfection, yielding truly delicious white wine that paid off handsomely. This twist of fate prompted the innkeeper to name his vineyard after the scurrilous black cat, and dogs were never again allowed in either his vineyard or the Electoral Castle Inn. The humped-up, frightened black cat logo is easily recognized on the shelves as Black Cat Riesling, among so many of the tasty, slightly sweet popular-priced white wines from this alluring landscape of Germany.

BOCKSBEUTEL: THE GOAT'S SCROTUM

In 1316 the von Steren family funded the construction of a hospital in Wurzburg, Germany, the capital city of the Franken winegrowing region. They called it the Burgerspital to the Holy Spirit and operated it with monks, who also tended its vineyards and made its wine. Patients and residents were rationed a tankard a day as long as they behaved themselves. If not, their wine was diluted with water, and if that failed to correct a problem, malcontents were cut off completely.

By the early 1800s the monks bottled their wine in short

squatty glass flasks called *Bocksbeutels*. There are several stories about the origin of this word. It may be a corruption of *Booksbudel* (sack to carry books), but a more popular notion is that *Bock* (a male goat) and *Beutel* (a purse) were combined to make the medieval term referring to a testicle sack. In either case, the heart-shaped bottle was utilitarian because monks could tie a string around the neck and carry it under their armpit much like a shoulder holster. Deftly reaching under their habit, they could take the occasional nip with none the wiser. In any case, the shape is a stark departure from the traditional long narrow German *Schlegelflashcen* (hock) bottles we see yet today, which still tempt jest as "horse medicine bottles."

All wines grown in the Franken region are now required to be packaged in Bocksbeutel flasks—a shape that is copyright protected by the European Union. The hospital serves today as a hospice for the elderly, and the wine estate still produces and markets wine under the Burgerspital Wurzburg label.

He who loves not wine,

women and song remains

a fool his whole life long.

—Johann Heinrich Voss, German poet and translator (1751–1826); also attributed to Martin Luther

SCHLOSS JOHANNISBERG: BETTER LATE THAN NEVER

The sweet nectar of every late harvest wine recalls the legend of the very first. During the latter half of the eighteenth century, prince-bishops ruled Germany with regal splendor. They micromanaged most every manner of everything, right down to when wine grapes were permitted to be harvested.

It was in 1775 that a particularly forgetful sovereign let the harvest proclamation slip by. Winegrowers waited and waited, becoming frantic as their grapes moved past peak ripeness. Bold to action, the monks of Schloss Johannisberg sent an emissary to secure permission from the prince-bishop to harvest their grapes. According to some accounts, the courier was detained by the attractions of a young lady. In any case, by the time the young man returned, Johannisberg's precious Riesling grapes had become infected with a gray mold the desperate vintners called

⚜ A Dangerous Game ⚜

THE SCIENTIFIC classification of the noble mold is *Botrytis cinerea*. Its dewatering effect enriches flavors and sugars but produces much less quantity and is also risky. Temperature and humidity have to be favorable or the mold becomes infectious and can ruin a crop with its rampant growth. Consequently, vintners must be judicious in how much of their grape harvest is held late, hoping for the famous gray mold to work its magic. Success is rewarded with classic wines that are understandably expensive.

Edelfäule, which is the same as the *pourriture noble* (noble mold) of the Sauternes district in Bordeaux. There was little choice for the monks but to make wine from the gray shriveled fruit. To their delight, the result was a sweet golden wine like none other before.

BULL'S BLOOD: TERRIFYING WINE

During the 1550s the Turkish ruler Suleiman the Magnificent prepared his siege of Eger Castle in the Beech Mountains of northern Hungary. The fortress was defended by two thousand soldiers and civilians led by Captain István Dobó against far more Turks. Miraculously, the Hungarians held their stations despite several weeks of repeated attacks on their walls. It was during this onslaught that Dobó authorized rations of red wine to maintain the strength and morale of his defenders. The story goes that wine streamed down the thirsty soldier's beards and armor, creating the notion among the enemy that the Hungarians were drinking bull's blood to give them superhuman strength. As a result, the Turks withdrew from the Eger fortress.

It was another two hundred years or so before the Eger winegrowers commercialized their red wine legend into bottles of the now famous Egri Bikavér (Bull's Blood of Eger). Under former Soviet rule, the Eger vineyards were replanted with lesser-quality vine varieties, which were easier to grow and produced larger crops. Since liberation, the region has continued to invest in and work back to traditions that made Egri Bikavér one of Hungary's most important wine exports.

PASS THE PORT, PLEASE!

British vintners in Portugal convene in regular brotherhood gatherings in the cities of Oporto and Vila Nova de Gaia. Typically, these are luncheon or dinner meetings held at a large round table during which ranking members conduct a business agenda. Meetings are concluded with a friendly test of the participants' palates with blind tastings of various vintages.

The tasty, sweet, heady red wine made in this part of Portugal is called Port throughout the wine world. Decanters of unidentified Port wine are always served to each participant by being "passed to the left," a tradition perhaps taken from British sailing jargon because the port side of a ship is the left side. Another curious explanation for this is that passing the wine with the left hand to the person on the left kept the right hand free to quickly reach for a sword should that be necessary.

Regardless, the tastings continue, with each decanter being passed clockwise until it returns to the host. Should the decanter become delayed for some reason, the host will typically ask the detainer, "Do you know the bishop of Norwich?" This is usually met with a prompt dispatch of the Port decanter on its way clockwise again, never directly across the table. If the delay continues, the host may call out again, "The bishop is a good fellow, but he never passes the Port!"

ON AND OFF THE WAGON

Before there were paved roads, a water wagon was used to wet down the dry summer dust. Similarly, people who were parched needed "water from the wagon" to wet down their thirst. Those trying to replace excessive booze consumption with water were thus called "on

the wagon." Anyone who went "off the wagon" was thus back into the booze again.

Abstinence from wine may not help you live longer, but it will sure seem like it.

—Gordon "Stan" Howell, professor of viticulture emeritus, Michigan State University

THE BITTER END

Long before wine was presented in glass bottles it was served directly from clay pots, wooden barrels, and such. All wines, reds in particular, will over time precipitate astringent and bitter sediments—or, in wine vernacular, "throw its lees." Thus, those unfortunate enough to get a cup of wine drawn too close to

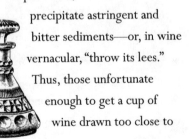

these dregs found tasting them to be "the bitter end."

While wine enthusiasts may choose to accept that account for the expression, there is another that relates to sailing. The ends of lines, ropes, and hawsers that are wound around the noose-like deadeyes of blocks, pulleys, and other fittings were traditionally separated strands that were woven into the main cordage to make a permanent loop. Sailors still refer to a loose strand as a "bitter end" that needs to be spliced back securely.

THREE SHEETS TO THE WIND

In the days of square-rigged tall ships, such as the magnificent China tea clippers of the mid-nineteenth century, there was extra caution taken with the amount of sail that would be unfurled during high winds. Captains would generally order

their uppermost sails, the royals and skysails, to remain furled to their yardarms in order to decrease leverage from strong gusts that threatened the breaking point of each mast. Heavy squalls and gales would then push relentlessly into the remaining three lower sheets, causing the ship to pitch and roll, which in turn made perfectly sober sailors stagger and stumble on the decks. Sailors returning from shore liberty who had consumed sufficient wine or spirits to reach a drunken wobbly stupor were thus referred to as being "three sheets to the wind."

I try not to drink too much. When I'm drunk I bite!

—Bette Midler, star of stage and screen

THE BEAUTY OF LONG LEGS

Some folks remain convinced that wine quality can be measured by the length of the legs formed by droplets that arise around the inside rim of a wineglass. According to convention, longer legs indicate better wine. When room temperature wine is poured into a cold glass, the alcohol and other volatile constituents are easily evaporated, creating long wine legs. But if the same wine is chilled before pouring, the resulting wine legs will be shorter. While some fine wines may well be long-legged beauties, it is not an exact science, and every experienced wine enthusiast can remember some tasty short-legged wines.

BOOZING IT UP

Several notions exist as to the origin of the word *booze* and its rather crude reference to excess drinking. The medieval English word *bouse* was taken from the Dutch and German *busen*, both meaning "drunk," although the German translation infers a bit of raucous revelry as well. Another idea is that the word comes from World War I–era demeaning slang that was derived from the sparkling wines grown in Bouzy vineyards in the Champagne region of France. Bouzy, however, is hardly booze. It has a noble heritage: Louis XIV personally selected it for his 1654 coronation in Champagne, and it has remained ever since a prime French bubbly.

SNEAKY PETE

There are St. Sneaky Pete's Day celebrations that include copious amounts of green beer consumption during which participants recount the most memorable sneaky jokes, tricks, and other underhanded wiles they have committed on others. As it relates to wine, Sneaky Pete was once the beverage of choice for cheap lechers to offer ladies reluctant to share their favors. Over time, the generally accepted use of the term *Sneaky Pete* was for cheap high-alcohol wine concealed in a paper bag that would result in a buzz sneaking up on drinkers after they had taken only a few quick chugs.

THE HEARTBREAK OF PLONK

Every seasoned wine veteran has heard of plonk. The French call white wine *vin blanc* and pronounce it "vawn blawnk." This was corrupted to *plawnk* or *plonk*, perhaps purposely, by American soldiers returning from World War II in Europe. It has since become a rather snobbish term meant to insult any modestly priced wine.

4

Founders and Fathers

W HEN NORSEMAN LEIF Erikson landed on the northern coastline of North America about a thousand years ago, one of his crewmen went ashore and ventured into the forest. It was dense with trees that were natural trellises for vines heavily laden with grapes. It was a discovery so profound that Erikson called the land Vineland.

The Europeans who followed nearly half a century later found much the same bounty—grapes that seemed to give promise for growing wine as they had in the Old World. But that hope was quickly dashed when they found that some of the native species, *Vitis labrusca* and *V. riparia*, among others, produced grapes that were sharply tart or had what

French settlers called *gout sauvage* (savage taste).

A far worse revelation was that repeated attempts to cultivate the more delicate and flavorful varieties of the time-honored European *Vitis vinifera* species vines were fruitless. Young vineyards died without apparent reason. It was a curious dilemma that went unsolved until the late 1800s.

Colonial settlers who had the means to buy imported French, German, and other European wines were usually aristocrats. Some of those who weren't so well healed were clergy, who kept their winegrowing faith by prayer and hard work. Some hopeful winegrowers were liberated convicts banished to the New World. The character and resolve of each make for some stimulating stories.

PENN'S WOODS

Perhaps Vineyard Street in the old Francisville area of Philadelphia may be the only remaining clue for people traveling through the area that was William Penn's vineyard more than three hundred years ago. Liberal Quaker beliefs got young Penn kicked out of the Puritans' Church of England. Because his father, a wealthy navy admiral, was politically connected, the adventurous young Penn was granted a huge land grant in the American colonies, which was to create opportunities for emigrating Quakers in the 1680s. The woodland territory stretched across the entire east–west reaches of British New World holdings and was called Pennsylvania, Latin for "Penns Woods."

One of Penn's early projects was to clear land for vineyards to make wine for colonial Quakers, who drank wine in moderation with meals and for worship in compliance with biblical teachings. The Francisville vineyard was thus the first planted in Pennsylvania, but it fared no better than other transplanted European vines, which died without any apparent cause.

BENJAMIN FRANKLIN: BAWDY BON VIVANT

As the American minister to France, Ben Franklin was a very popular invite for the frequent free-flowing soirees thrown by Parisian aristocrats. His love of their wine and food and his charming demeanor, especially with the ladies, established him as a fascinating and witty bon vivant, who was always at the ready with entertaining comments and quips.

Among the many accounts of his risqué character are those that wax eloquent about delicate subjects. He once proposed drinking wine infused with dried rhubarb and roses to perfume the effects of foul flatulence. An especially articulate abbot sang a drinking song that, in jest, accused Franklin of starting the American Revolution so that French wine could replace English tea. The American minister responded by sending the cleric a letter that included this passage:

> *To confirm you in your piety, and recognition of Divine Providence, reflect on the position Providence has given the elbow. Man, who was destined to drink wine, has to be able to carry the glass to his mouth. If the elbow had been placed closer to the hand, the forearm would have been too short to bring the glass to the mouth; if it had been closer to the shoulder, the forearm would have been so long that it would have carried the glass beyond the mouth. Let us*

then adore, glass in hand, this
beneficent Wisdom. Let us adore
and drink.

THOMAS JEFFERSON: MONICELLO MYSTERY

There can be little question that
Thomas Jefferson was the most
influential wine patriot during the
founding days of American
independence. Out of privileged
Welsh descent, his first appreciation
for wine in the New World was
probably as an imbibing student at
the College of William & Mary in
Williamsburg, Virginia, where he
graduated with top honors in
mathematics, philosophy, and law in
1762 at the age of nineteen.

Accepted to the Virginia bar in
1767, his legal and political prowess
quickly earned him prominence,
resulting in his principal authorship
of the Declaration of Independence
and an appointment as governor of
Virginia. He was an expert on
many subjects and had a refined
taste for food and wine. In fact, he
built several wine cellars in his
home, Monticello (little mountain),
and the cellars remain up close and
personal for visitors to see.

In 1784 Congress appointed
Jefferson minister to France,
relieving his good friend Benjamin
Franklin of the post. Jefferson was
a popular figure at the French
court, although considerably more
formally disposed than the ribald
character of Franklin. The ministry
was the perfect opportunity for
him to enhance his already
impressive wine knowledge. His
travels to many of the famed
French chateaux and domaines are
recorded via his signature in visitor
gold books. Jefferson's good
reputation among the French was

enhanced because he spoke their language and had vivid enthusiasm for their wine.

Jefferson returned to America in 1789 eager to plant European vines at Monticello, in Charlottesville, Virginia. Several attempts ended in the same mysterious failure that had vexed generations of previous hopefuls. He hired European viticulture experts, who also failed to grow the coveted Old World vines. Winegrowing was an obsession that led Jefferson to the brink of bankruptcy, but he never doubted America as a nation that could grow wine as good as France.

Wine being among the earliest luxuries in which we indulge ourselves,

it is desirable it should be made here and we have every soil, aspect & climate of the best wine countries . . . these South West mountains, having a S.E. aspect, and abundance of lean & meager spots of stony & red soil, without sand, resembling extremely the Cote of Burgundy from Chambertin to Montrachet, where the famous wines of Burgundy are made.

—Thomas Jefferson, third president of the United States

GEORGE WASHINGTON: MATCHING MUTTON WITH MADEIRA

Having enjoyed many wine experiences in France, Thomas Jefferson and Benjamin Franklin could speak of wine with authority. Jefferson, in particular, often suggested new and different types of wine to his political peers. Glasses were held high in toasts that were, depending on the times, either solemn or jovial.

My manner of living is plain and I do not mean to be put out of it. A glass of wine and a bit of mutton are always ready.

—George Washington, letter to George W. Fairfax (June 1786)

George Washington enjoyed sweet German whites and some superior Bordeaux reds, both doubtlessly Jefferson suggestions. In particular, the first American president liked rich, nutty high-alcohol Madeira, which probably soothed his aching teeth, a curse he endured most of his adult life.

JOHN HANCOCK: WINE SMUGGLER?

It was a crafty businessman and politician who was first to endorse the American Declaration of Independence with his iconic signature. Having inherited the House of Hancock importing company from his uncle in 1764, John Hancock was well versed in the business of bringing manufactured goods into Boston. As political and economic tension grew with Britain,

Hancock became an activist in the movement against colonial "taxation without representation." A call for a boycott of British

✺ *Rainwater Madeira* ✺

MOST OF the wine imported to the American colonies was Madeira, made from Malvasia and Sercial grapes grown on the Portuguese island of Madeira. A heady sweet wine fortified with brandy, Madeira was actually baked in steamy rooms that purposely oxidized grape flavors into a rich nutty character. It cost less than other European wines, mostly because King Charles II excluded Madeira wines from a curious regulation that required wines bound for the colonies to be shipped in a British ship from a British harbor. It was also cheaper in that the higher alcohol meant that just a little could give a quick buzz after a hard day of building a new country.

One particular shipment of Madeira was curiously a bit more delicate in flavor and body than previous orders. Investigation back on the Isle of Madeira found that the *bungs* (plug closures) on some *pipes* (large wooden barrels) of Madeira were inadvertently left open at the quay in Madeira before being loaded onto the ship and were thus inadvertently topped-up by rainwater. The guilty vintners fully expected to receive complaints, until they learned that the Americans actually preferred this style. Hence, future shipments were purposely ameliorated with fresh rainwater and proudly labeled as "Rainwater Madeira," as it remains yet today.

imports eventually led to the famous Boston Tea Party, after which smuggling became a rather common method to avoid paying import duty to England.

Hancock was wealthy, among the richest of Bostonians, and, as a Whig member of the Massachusetts House of Representatives, was both commercially and politically well connected. In 1768, his brig, the *Lydia*, came under suspicion by British "tidesmen," who were agents for duty payment. They came aboard to inspect the cargo but were turned away by the crew, and charges were filed. The charges were dropped by Attorney General Jonathan Sewell, who ruled that the English officials had not obtained a proper search warrant.

A month later another of John Hancock's transport ships, with the precocious name of *Liberty*, arrived in Boston Harbor with a hold thought to have been fully loaded with Madeira wine. When the tidesmen came to inventory the ship the next day, they found only about one quarter of the ship's capacity filled with wine. Hancock paid the duty for what they had found and no more. He was charged with smuggling, but his clever attorney, John Adams, succeeded in getting the charges dropped.

PADRE JUNÍPERO SERRA: THE ROYAL ROAD

The very first vineyards in California were quite literally rooted in the church, with vines delivered by Spanish conquistadors. General José de Gálvez ordered fortified settlements to be constructed northward from the *Baja* (lower) California coast to shield the territory from English explorers and Russian fur traders. Captain Gaspar de Portolá was assigned to lead the operation, and in 1769, he set out from Baja with a garrison of soldiers and a devout Catholic priest, Junípero Serra.

Men are like wine—some turn to vinegar, but the best improve with age.

—Pope John XXIII

Their first settlement, Mission San Diego, was constructed that same year and planted with what may have been the variety Monica, also known as Mission vines, which Serra had brought along to produce wine for both Mass and table. Unlike plantings of Old World vines in the eastern colonies, Serra's vineyard lived. He carried his vines to five more missions as the El Camino Real (The Royal Road) was continued. The Spanish eventually built twelve missions, the last one being Padre José Altimira's at Sonoma in 1823. These small outposts served well not only as sanctuaries but also as the earliest winegrowing experiments in California, forming the basis for today's commercial vineyards.

JOSEPH CHAPMAN: PIRATE VINTNER

How colorful is it that the first commercial California vintner was a pirate? Joseph Chapman was a Bostonian who made his way to California only to be shanghaied by Argentine privateer Hippolyte de Bouchard. On an 1818 raid gone sour, Joseph Chapman was taken prisoner by the Spanish in Monterey. After his release, Chapman sought out the Santa Yñez and San Gabriel missions, where he found work with Father Junípero Serra and became fascinated and well schooled in growing grapes and making wine. It was there that he became known as José Huero (Blond Joe).

◈ The Left Hand of God ◈

THE MENTION of winegrowing in upstate New York brings to mind the jaw-dropping beauty of the austere Finger Lakes Region landscape between the cities of Rochester and Syracuse. More than ten thousand years ago, glaciers carved a series of deep lakes that are configured much like the fingers on a left hand (a quick check of a map will readily confirm this). Locals, however, insist that this is where God rested his hand to bless his magnificent earthly creation.

By 1826 he had saved enough money to acquire property in Los Angeles and planted several thousand vines. Even at a scant five pounds of fruit per vine, his production would have made around fifteen hundred gallons of wine each vintage and probably more, certainly far more than what he could have drunk himself. From that it is assumed that Joseph Chapman either sold or traded his wine and was thus a commercial vintner—the first in California.

THE REVEREND WILLIAM BOSTWICK: ANGLICAN INSPIRATION

New York State's wine mentor was one of God's messengers, Father William Bostwick. He was rector of St. James Episcopal Church in Hammondsport on the southernmost shore of Keuka Lake, the "thumb" of the Finger Lakes. Because he needed wine for the Sunday Eucharist, he decided to try making his own. Given the well-publicized failures of accomplished eastern New World winegrowers who worked with European *V. vinifera* vines, Bostwick decided to start with native American varieties, which he planted behind his church in 1829. The quality of his sacramental wine inspired commercial winemakers to plant vineyards on the banks of all the Finger Lakes, and thus the New York State wine industry was born.

Go thy way, eat thy bread with joy, and drink thy wine with a merry heart; for God have accepted thy works.

—Ecclesiastes 9:7

GEORGE YOUNT: NAPA PIONEER

The quaint little village of Yountville at the southern end of Napa Valley was named in honor of nineteenth-century wine pioneer George Yount. In 1804, when the boy was ten, his family left North Carolina for Missouri. As a young man, Yount headed farther west, settling in Santa Fe, New Mexico, and working his way into a lucrative distilling business, which eventually suffered ruin due to a crooked partner.

He arrived in Sonoma, California, in 1831, hunting and trapping among Native Americans as a rare white man in the region. He found work at the new Sonoma Mission and, five years later, was awarded a Mexican homestead grant in the Napa Valley, where he built the first log house in the region. Friendly Indians looked upon the dwelling, complete with an interior hearth and chimney, in utter amazement.

A French visitor, a veteran of Napoleon's campaigns, may have influenced Yount to plant Mission vines for his personal use next to the log cabin circa 1840. A monument in Yountville today proudly recalls the memory of George Yount, Napa Valley's first winegrower.

COUNT AGOSTON HARASZTHY: WHERE IT ALL BEGAN

Up until the mid-1800s, the best California wines were grown from Spanish vines planted in the

Franciscan mission vineyards along the El Camino Real, which stretched from San Diego to Sonoma. But the quality of wine from these vineyards paled in comparison to those from Mother Europe.

In 1861 Count Agoston Haraszthy, a Hungarian ex-patriot living in Sonoma, convinced California Governor John Downey to provide travel funds for a trip to visit the grand European vineyards. A proviso in the deal was that Haraszthy would return with cuttings that could be propagated, planted, and cultivated by the latest winegrowing methods. He agreed, complied, and shipped several hundred noble *V. vinifera* vines back to Sonoma, although difficulties in labeling and handling resulted in years of puzzling confusion in identifying just which variety was which.

⟡ *Where It All Ended* ⟡

HARASZTHY'S SUCCESS led to wild spending on the design of his Buena Vista Winery estate, which resulted in bankruptcy and his fleeing from financial woes. His demise is thought to have come in Brazil, where reports indicated he lost his life in the jaws of an Amazon beast.

Some vines expected to yield white grapes produced reds, and vice versa; it took a long while to straighten out the mess.

Nevertheless, Haraszthy had accomplished introducing classic Old World vines to California, vines that thrived in western America because the phylloxera root lice did not exist there, as it did in the vineyards of Jefferson and others in the east. Tourists visiting the old stone Buena Vista Winery can see the original Haraszthy vineyard site nearby, in front of which is an archway sign inscribed, "Here Is Where It All Began."

JUAN CEDRÓN: ARGENTINA'S MISSION VINEYARDS

There is evidence that winegrowing was brought from Spain to the Río de la Plata near Buenos Aires in the early 1540s. But the first recorded commercial vineyard is credited to Juan Cedrón, a displaced Chilean priest who planted Spanish Mission vine varieties near the Argentine city of Santiago del Estero in 1556. Thus, the first Argentine wines predate those of the El Camino Real mission trail in California by more than two hundred years.

The *Phylloxera vastatrix* root

louse did not exist in South America as it did in eastern North America, meaning Old World *V. vinifera* vines were able to thrive. By 1560 Argentina had budding wine industries in the Cuyo and Mendoza plateau regions on the slopes of the Andes.

Albariño and Torrontés became well established as the premier white wine varieties, but there was no clear favorite for reds. Tempranillo vines made acceptable red wines, although light in style because the arid soils required irrigation. Perhaps the best of them were grown in the La Rioja district, named for the large winegrowing region in Spain where that variety is widely cultivated.

An essential development of Argentine winegrowing commenced in 1868 when Provincial Governor Domingo Sarmiento contracted Professor Miguel Pouget to import some French vines.

Among these were Malbec vines, one of the five major vines cultivated by the great Bordeaux chateau estates. Growing problems have since rendered Malbec less important for red wine blending in Bordeaux. But Argentina *terroir* (combination of soil and climate) is more agreeable for Malbec vines, and the grape is now the signature variety of the country.

PADRE FRANCISCO COPIAPÓ: CHILE'S PERFECT TERROIR

Notwithstanding rather frequent devastating earthquakes, Chile has perhaps the most perfect terroir for winegrowing on earth. It differs from California in being a narrow strip of land moderated by Pacific coastal breezes and cradled by the towering Andes Mountains.

None of the common vineyard pests blighting other winegrowing nations have ever invaded Chile. As a result, Chilean vines do not require grafting on resistant rootstocks and require minimal cultivation remedies. A case could be made that Chilean wines are perhaps more pure and less affected by grafted roots than those grown from the same varieties in Mother Europe or anywhere else.

Among the first to plant vines in Chile was Padre Francisco de Aguirre Copiapó. Subsequently, a commercial vineyard was planted in 1554 by Diego García de Cáceres. Varieties such as Albillo, Monastrell, Muscat Blanc, and Torontel (same as the Spanish Torrontés), along with the Mission vine, prompted the Chilean wine industry to grow rapidly, so much so that wine imports from Spain declined. King Philip II trumped that with a decree prohibiting further vineyard plantings in his Chilean colony so that it would continue to import wines from Spain. But his statute was largely ignored, and Chile's winegrowers continued planting vineyards.

In 1851, Don Silvestre Ochagavía Echazarreta brought the first classic French and Italian *V. vinifera* vines to Chile and, as a result, became the patriarch of the nation's modern era of winegrowing.

LANDRIEN AND DE RIVEAU: AUSTRALIA'S CONVICT LEGACY

It was the arrival of some former French prisoners that started

grape growing in Australia. They arrived in the late 1780s and promptly settled at Port Jackson, which is now Sydney Harbor. Thanks to the convict's essential French thirst for wine, vines were eventually brought in from South America for planting in New South Wales. A decade later, their success with winegrowing encouraged the founding of several private vineyards. Within another decade, more French convicts were brought to the area. Among these were Antoine Landrien and Francois de Riveau, who taught vine growing and winemaking and provided the spark that ignited Aussie wine enthusiasm to commercial production.

JAMES BUSBY: RAISING THE BAR

Native Englishman James Busby could be called the Thomas Jefferson of New Zealand. He left England in 1824 for Australia, where he planted Old World vines and wrote several treatises for commercial viticulture and winemaking.

Busby moved to New Zealand in 1832 and expended much of the same pioneering effort in planting Old World vines and publishing winegrowing techniques as he had in Australia. He made his first wine in 1834, and a good share of that vintage was made into sweet quaffs preferred by British soldiers and other British ex-pats in New Zealand at the time. A year later, he was called on to turn his authorship talents toward writing the Declaration of Independence for New Zealand, which succeeded in turning back a threat of annexation from France.

5

The Allure of New World Wine

EUROPEAN IMMIGRANTS DIDN'T like the wine made from the bounty of native vines found in America. Most were literally sour grapes with tart acidity and crude flavors. The obvious alternative was to plant classic Old World vines. But they always died rather mysteriously, as if having had a curse put on them in Europe. Unfortunately, the evil demon was in America: a devilish phylloxera louse hidden

in the soil. Native vine roots were impervious to it, but European vines were not. Despite this cruel discrimination, there were some steadfast believers that commercial winegrowing from native vines in the central and eastern states was viable. This chapter embraces some of those remarkable people who would not be denied.

INDIANA: HOOSIER RHINELAND

For a few years Indiana was one of the largest winegrowing states in America. In 1796, Jean Jacques

Dufour, an experienced winegrower, emigrated to America from the village of Vevey in the Vaud wine region of Switzerland. His quest was to grow wine grapes for what was reputed in Europe as a shortage of wine after America's successful revolt from England. He toured several vineyards in the eastern states, including those planted by Thomas Jefferson at Monticello in Virginia. Jefferson's failure to successfully grow Old World vines there prompted a suggestion that Dufour try his pursuit farther west. Dufour complied and, by 1801, had established a small vineyard in Kentucky but gave this up in favor of even better terroir prospects across the Ohio River in Indiana.

An 1802 act of Congress extended Dufour credit to buy twenty-five hundred acres of Indiana hillside land on the banks of the Ohio. Fully aware of the failure of European vines in America, he planted Cape vines, native to South Africa. They flourished, and Dufour's success attracted other Swiss immigrants, who bought parcels of his land holdings and thus created an entire Swiss community.

The new settlement was named Vevay in 1813, an obvious but misspelled namesake for their Swiss homeland town of Vevey. A year later, Vevay became the county seat of Switzerland County, two years before Indiana became a state. By this time, thousands of acres of vineyard had been planted on terraces overlooking the Ohio River, and boats carried wines in quantity downstream to New Orleans and out to major eastern markets.

Dufour's vineyard region grew sufficiently enough to become known as "the Little Rhineland" and one of the largest single winegrowing locales in America. Success was comparatively short lived, however, as a blight of mildew and pests wiped out all the vineyards in the entire region after some particularly hot and humid summers.

---ᗅᗅᗅ---

OHIO: BUCKEYE BUBBLY

The Iroquois word for "great river" is *ohio*, which became the official state name when the territory was admitted to the Union in 1803. A decade later, wealthy attorney Nicholas Longworth planted his first vineyards near Cincinnati. Longworth spent decades experimenting. His plantings of Old World *Vitis vinifera* vines died, just as they had across all of young America. Cape vines brought up from Indiana were successful, but Catawba vines expressed a more agreeable white wine flavor profile that was much more delicate than most other New World varieties.

Longworth settled on making Catawba wine commercially in the traditional German method of pressing crushed grapes and then slowly fermenting the resulting juice at cool temperatures. The result was a fresh pinkish white wine, which the increasing number of German immigrants into the Ohio Valley purchased repeatedly.

In 1842, a batch of Catawba wine inadvertently bottled before fermentation had completely finished bubbled forth, much like what French friar Dom Pérignon had experienced in the Champagne region more than two hundred years earlier. Expanding on that idea, Longworth hired some Champagne winemakers from France and commenced making "Ohio Champagne" from his Catawba grapes. The first vintage ended in disaster, as more than forty thousand bottles exploded from the traditional *méthod champenoise* process. Undaunted, Longworth's wealth permitted him to

acquire better bottles, hire new technical expertise, and move forward with his sparkling wine vision. By the mid-1850s, his Ohio Champagne was supplying a burgeoning demand. Poet Henry Wadsworth Longfellow compared it to the sparkling wine made from the Verzenay and Sillery vineyards in Champagne. The following is from his 1854 "Birds of Passage (Flight the First)":

> *Very good in its way*
> *Is the Verzenay*
> *Or the Sillery soft and creamy;*
> *But Catawba wine*
> *Has a taste more divine,*
> *More dulcet, delicious, and dreamy.*

At the time of Nicholas Longworth's death in 1863, Ohio River winemakers were supplying more than a third of the wine grown in America. But that success was threatened by the Civil War, already two years old, and a looming Temperance movement leaking south from Canada. But the final blows to Longworth's business were invasions of black rot and downy mildew, which struck vineyards across the Midwest.

MISSOURI: WINE GATEWAY TO CALIFORNIA

French Jesuits made the first Missouri wine at a seminary they established near St. Louis in 1823. They were soon outnumbered by the Germans who followed, most of whom were beer drinkers and thus beer makers. Some of the Germans were winemakers, although they didn't come close to the scale of beer production that was exemplified by the Anheuser and Busch families.

❧ *Norton's Revelation* ❧

THE NORTON vine was discovered by Dr. D. N. Norton in 1820 while walking through his Richmond, Virginia, garden. It was also called Norton's Virginia and Cynthiana. The visual aspect of the vine was curiously more European than the typical American vines growing in his area. The wine made from its dark red grapes was decidedly Old World in character and was a revelation in red wine quality from American grapes.

Jacob Fugger was among the first Prussian immigrants to plant vines in Missouri, near the town of Hermann in 1843. Another wine pioneer was Gustave Koerner, who told of offering a taste of wine from his Norton vines to a visitor from Germany, who was so impressed he was sure it was Burgundy.

Theodore Hilgard, who emigrated from Zweibrücken, turned his Norton grapes into a wine he egotistically called Hilgardsberger. Hilgard's son Eugene became proficient in viticulture and eventually moved on to the University of California at Berkeley as a professor of agriculture. Young Hilgard later championed the importance of research, which led to the development of the Viticulture and Enology Department at the University of California at Davis, which has since served in the rapid growth of California winegrowing.

THE AMANA COMMUNITY: SOCIALLY INSPIRED

Anyone who has driven Iowa's highways knows that its agriculture fame is from vast fields of grain, not vineyards. Nevertheless, the Hawkeye State has a fascinating wine heritage.

Iowa was admitted to the Union in 1846, its name taken from the Sioux word *ioway*, meaning "river." Eight years later, a spiritually driven communal sect, calling themselves the Community of True Inspiration, arrived from New York State and purchased about twenty-five thousand acres of prairie land twenty miles or so southwest of Cedar Rapids. That was the beginning of the Amana Society Community. It was a socialist commune in every way: totally self-sufficient and strictly following the *Amana* (remain

true) dictum, taken from the Bible by the Lutheran Germans who had founded the clan a century earlier.

The society owned everything it had and made everything it needed. Its people worked in return for food, wine, shelter, and other basic needs. Amana's *Weinmeister* supervised the planting of vines and the making of wines. Each family had assigned tasks in the vineyards and cellars, and every vintage was rationed to twenty gallons per man and twelve for women. This was supplemented with wine made from *Piestengel* ("pie plant," or "rhubarb," a pinkish stalk that made both pie and wine).

The Amana Society remained this way for some eighty years, until national Prohibition and the Great Depression came down with a devastating impact on the vines and wines. As a result, their vineyards were pulled out, and more than nineteen thousand gallons of wine were dumped.

Jokesters quipped that afterward, Mississippi River fish suffered from Amana hangovers.

Impoverished, the society voted to abandon socialism and join the rest of America in capitalism. Members became stockholders of the Amana commonwealth, and with the repeal of Prohibition in 1933, some ventured into commercial winemaking. That was immediately bridled when Iowa became one of nineteen states to adopt total control of all wholesale and retail wine distribution. Fortunately, legislation has not been a serious hurdle for a new generation of Iowa winegrowers, who have succeeded in resurrecting prairie vineyards.

The largest restaurant wine cellar in the world is at Bern's Steak House in Tampa, Florida. Diners enjoy prime beef while sitting above the more than ninety thousand bottles held in the crypt below. The restaurant has another five hundred thousand or so in nearby storage!

ILLINOIS: ALONS EN AMERIQUE

The city of Joliet, Illinois, celebrates the 1670s exploration of Louis Joliet, who, along with Catholic missionary Jacques Marquette, embarked on a journey designed to find a shortcut to Asian markets. The Northwest Passage took them south from Quebec to the Mississippi River into *illinois*, an

Algonquin word meaning "land of superior warriors." That Joliet and Marquette were both native Frenchmen, and the latter also a cleric, would entertain the notion that they were familiar with wine and sensitive to areas where vines might grow. If the men had such aspirations, there is no record of them.

Illinois winegrowing was, however, eventually established by another Frenchman—Étienne Cabet, a vocal objector of French postrevolution government. Cabet advocated another revolt in the name of Marxist socialism. He wrote an 1847 article called "Allons en Amerique" (Come to America), published in *Le Populaire*, then a contemporary socialist journal, which invited people gifted in various crafts and trades to a utopian self-sufficient settlement in Texas he called Icaria, for which there seems to be no translation. While there was plenty of inexpensive land and political isolation in the new

Icaria, the Texan commune fell short of prosperity. Three years later, Cabet moved the Icarians to Nauvoo, Illinois, on the Mississippi River. Hardy Concord vines were planted, and today wines are made from grapes harvested from the original 1851 vineyard site in Nauvoo State Park.

Nauvoo had been settled by prophet Joseph Smith and his followers, who built their first Mormon temple more than a decade earlier. By the time Cabet arrived, however, Nauvoo (Hebrew for "beautiful plantation") was a political battlefield that was largely abandoned. Smith had been murdered in 1844, after which Brigham Young led the community to Salt Lake City. Thus, Étienne Cabet found plenty of empty homes in which to restart the communal utopia. The next generation of Icarians planted more than six hundred acres of vines, supplying over three dozen wineries that grew in tandem with the Nauvoo blue cheese industry.

⋆ *The Wedding of Wine and Cheese* ⋆

THE NAUVOO community annually celebrates the legend of a French shepherd boy who found a blue mold growing on cheese he had left in a cave days before and thus discovered blue cheese. The "wedding ceremony" is conducted by a magistrate, who reads a marriage certificate and then places it between some wine, which is the bride, and some blue cheese, which is the groom. The happy couple sits atop a wine barrel. With that union declared, the festivities of the annual wine and cheese celebration begin.

WIPEOUT! UNCOVERING THE PHYLLOXERA SCOURGE

Conventional wisdom has America at fault for the *Phylloxera vastatrix*, a blight of root lice that invaded the vineyards of Europe. This is not entirely true: The messenger must take some of the blame. Eager academics at the Botanical Gardens in England imported some native North American grapevines for study during the early 1860s, unaware that the roots carried a microscopic louse. Most North American native species of *V. vinifera* are impervious to the tiny

pest, but the classic *V. vinifera* vines manicured in the great European wine vineyards were not. Phylloxera was initially discovered in the southern Rhone Valley in 1862, when some vines died mysteriously. No degree of vineyard rank or pedigree was spared. Aristocratic as well as common estates were undermined by the louse, which rampantly devoured the vineyards' roots. After several years of denial, the French government finally acknowledged the calamity.

An offer of thirty thousand gold francs was made for anyone who could come up with a viable solution to curb the disease. As would be expected, there were a bevy of bizarre suggestions. One included the flooding of vineyards with water to drown out the phylloxera, a curious notion given that many European

vineyards were situated upon hillsides. The devout faithful proposed sprinkling holy water from Lourdes on vines and praying that divine intervention would ward off the devilish infection. The French army agreed to collect urine from soldiers to pour on the vineyard soil, convinced that the stench would stem the rapid advance of the pest. Unfortunately, these and other attempts were ineffective. As vineyard after vineyard was lost to the devastation, there was, of course, a diminishing wine supply to fill demand. Nearly three quarters of French wine production was lost by 1889. By the end of World War I, the European wine industry was virtually lost.

The only practical solution was the use of American roots upon which the Cabernet Sauvignon, Chardonnay, Pinot Noir, Riesling, Nebbiolo, Sangiovese, and other classic *V. vinifera* varieties could be grafted for European vineyard replanting. Old World winegrowers had difficulty swallowing the idea, and the cost of buying roots from a wine-ignorant country condemned for the scourge to begin with was a sour prospect. In addition, the enormous costs to replant and the years-long wait for young vines to mature sufficiently for growers to make marketable wine were difficult to accept. But there was little choice. The classic irony continues because European vineyards still live on American roots.

WASHINGTON STATE ERUPTS WITH WINE

In 1825 Hudson's Bay Company traders at Fort Vancouver were among the first to plant vines in

❧ Texas Saves Europe's Vineyards ❧

DURING THE mid-1800s, Thomas Volney Munson's vineyard was replete with dozens of native American vine varieties propagated for studies to create hybrids designed to resist the disease, pests, and harsh weather existing on his large Denison, Texas, estate.

The only viable answer to the *Phylloxera vastatrix* root louse epidemic in Europe was grafting on resistant roots; thus, huge shipments of New World rootstocks were shipped to Europe. Vines from Munson's estate thus supplied the first roots on which the classic *V. vinifera* scions were grafted, which saved the European wine industry. He was subsequently awarded the prestigious Agriculture Soldier of Merit by the French Legion of Honor.

the state of Washington. Decades later, after the Gold Rush quieted down, German and Italian settlers planted vineyards in the Walla Walla area. Prohibition arrived in Washington two years earlier than in most other states, and thus commercial winegrowing came to an abrupt halt in 1917.

After the repeal of Prohibition, Washington State grape growers turned to native *Vitis labrusca* vine types, such as Concord and Niagara, which were grown primarily for sweet wines, grape juice, and other ancillary products. NAWICO and Pommerelle were among the first wineries to open for business in 1934.

In the 1950s, Dr. Walter Clore, a Washington State University (WSU) professor, commenced research and trials with some of the first Old World *V. vinifera* vine varieties. He encouraged a group of colleagues at WSU to make homemade wines from his grapes. Success further encouraged them to pool resources and found the Associated Vintners winery, which later became the Columbia Winery.

That was followed by a merging of the NAWICO and Pommerelle wineries into what is now Château Ste. Michelle. While both of these firms continue operations in Woodinville, a suburb of Seattle, most of the Washington State vineyards are located on the warm desert-like plains east of the Cascades in Walla Walla, Yakima, and along the Columbia River. With sufficient irrigation, these environs match up well with native Bordeaux varieties such as Merlot and Cabernet Sauvignon, both of which have been leaders in bringing remarkable wine quality notoriety to the state. The eruption of Mount St. Helens had little effect on the expansion of Washington winegrowing; indeed,

Beguiling Burgundy

THE 1975 vintage of Eyrie Vineyards Pinot Noir took top honors at the Gault-Millau Wine Olympics in France, besting all Burgundies in competition. It stunned the French—and especially the highly respected Burgundian winegrower Robert Drouhin. He demanded a rematch and won, albeit with a much older Chambolle-Musigny (1959), which was priced several times higher than Eyrie's second-place Oregon Pinot.

growth followed, with hundreds of new wineries cropping up at a rate that has led the nation.

~~~

OREGON: AMERICA'S BURGUNDY

It wasn't until after World War II that several visionaries pursued serious commercial winegrowing in Oregon. In 1961 Richard Sommer opened the doors of his Hillcrest Vineyard winery near Roseburg, in the southern part of the state. Taking the idea further was David Lett, a Californian who

was keen on the virtues of the Willamette Valley for a cooler climate, more conducive to Pinot Noir viticulture than that in much of California.

Conventional wisdom in the 1960s was that only France's Burgundy region could make sense

of the persnickety character of its native Pinot Noir. The best Burgundies came from vines that were cultivated to yield small crops of tiny berries that were packed with rich flavor, peaking only at a precise point of ripeness. Pinot wines from Lett's Eyrie Vineyards soon started impressing enthusiasts and experts across the country— and even in Burgundy. As would be expected, many other vintners came to Oregon to try their hand with the elusive Pinot Noir.

It's a naïve domestic Burgundy without any breeding, but I believe you will be amused by its presumption.

—James Thurber, cartoon in the *New Yorker*

6

Movers and Shakers

Slow development of the wine industry in tandem with an abundance of grain served to fashion young America into a brew- and spirits-drinking country. The Prohibition movement stymied U.S. winegrowing even further, as it did in Australia, New Zealand, Argentina, and Chile. World wars and economic depressions also served to cripple both wine production and consumer demand.

Despite such overwhelming hurdles, New World winegrowing has not only survived but thrived. A staggering number of commercial wine producers have risen since the 1960s, and wine enthusiasts no longer have to depend on Europe for fine vintages. Consumers can stock their cellars from thousands of wine offerings from the Americas and Down Under. New World wine consumption has grown such that it might now be considered wine culture. Some of the giant megastores offer several

hundred wines made from the same variety. We see and hear about wine everywhere—wine and health, wine and food, wine and travel, wine and most anything—and some wines are given Picasso-like homage in the media. This chapter features some fascinating characters key to the remarkable rise of non-European wines to global esteem.

LELAND STANFORD: MEGA ENTREPRENEUR

Born, raised, and educated in New York State, Leland Stanford practiced law in Wisconsin before moving to California in 1852 to join his brothers in several business ventures. With the Gold

Rush economy booming, Stanford was co-founder of the Central Pacific Railroad in 1861 and quickly became a tycoon. A year later, he was elected to a two-year term as the eighth governor of California. Continuing as president of Central Pacific, he directed construction of the first transcontinental railway and swung the hammer that drove in the historic golden spike that finished the project at Promontory, Utah, in 1869.

In 1881 Stanford added winegrowing to his impressive accomplishments, perhaps a curious move for a veteran of industry and politics. His brother

joined his Great Vina Ranch venture, which grew to cultivate more than thirty-five hundred acres of vineyard, the largest single plot of vines in the world at that time. That same year they founded two wineries: the Stanford Brothers Winery and the Great Vina Winery, both in Alameda County. It was a statement that California was becoming a player in the world of making wine, and it doubtlessly turned some heads in Europe.

Leland Stanford became a senator in 1885 and founded Stanford University in 1891. The university's very first student was future president Herbert Hoover.

THE WENTE FAMILY: CALIFORNIA WINE INNOVATORS

It is rare to find five generations of a family still in business. Wente Vineyards is a rare example; it's the single oldest continually

operating family-owned wine estate in America.

In 1883, Carl Wente settled in Livermore Valley, a warm, dry locale east of San Francisco and much different from the cold climate in his native Hannover, Germany. Having worked at the Charles Krug Winery in the Napa Valley, he knew how to make good wine. What he didn't know was that he had relocated to an area prone to earthquakes and tremors. Carl began a quest for top-quality vines, acquiring elite Cabernet Sauvignon cuttings from First Growth Château Margaux in Bordeaux.

While Carl was busy building the business side of the winery, his son, Ernest, patiently managed the vineyard, spending years

carefully cataloging the performance of the Margaux Cabernets and other vine stocks brought to Livermore from France. The best were eventually sent to the University of California at Davis (UCD) for propagation, to further improve commercial viticulture for the entire industry. Although given numerical identities at UCD, they were later popularly referred to as the "Old Wente" clones.

Karl Wente (who spelled his name with a *K*) was a third-generation grower who championed another ambition for his family's wine estate. His work figured into the design and testing of mechanized viticulture in most every manner, from planting to cultivation, irrigation, and harvesting. His views were reflected in the winery too. The use of cooling jackets on stainless-steel tanks for controlling the temperature of fermentation was one of Karl's ideas that is now employed throughout the wine industry worldwide. A 5.7 Richter Scale earthquake hit the Livermore area in 1980, leaving some Wente stainless-steel tanks looking like large twisted drink cans. Wente ingenuity developed shock-absorbing springs to support new tanks.

Fourth-generation scions Eric, Philip, and Carolyn are, yet again, unlike any of their forebears; these inventive developers and marketers pioneered California wine exports in the 1980s and 1990s. Under their direction, the estate has succeeded in becoming one of California's larger premium wine producers and one of America's most far-reaching global wine suppliers.

Fifth-generation Karl Wente has now taken root in the family firm and, like his great-great-grandfather, stands tall in the demand for top quality.

There are by some estimates approximately ten thousand varieties of grape vines in the world, an interesting number because some varieties, such as Pinot Gris and Sangiovese, are known by different names depending on where they are grown. In any event, only about 1 percent of these make up the greatest share of the twenty million or so acres of commercial vineyards. Grapes are thus the single largest producers of fruit. Spain has the most vineyards, with about 2.9 million acres. Next are France and Italy, each with around 2.0 million acres. Turkey is estimated at 1.4 million acres; China has 1.2 million; and the United States, 1.0 million. Much of Turkey's large expanse of vineyards produces table grapes, although wine is grown there due to a free Islamic culture.

LEFRANC'S BACCHANALS

Etienne Thee was a farmer in Bordeaux, France, before arriving in California to find gold. When that didn't pan out, he started a winery in the town of Los Gatos, near San Jose, in 1852. Native Frenchmen of that time often named their wine estates after people or places back home, but curiously, Thee took the name of Almaden, which translates from the medieval Spanish Moorish Arabic as "the field."

Thee's daughter had eyes for Charles Lefranc, also a Frenchman, who was an accomplished tailor. Marriage

into the family led him to quickly educate himself in the viticultural arts and spur his natural talent for winemaking, which promised far greater rewards than fashioning clothes. Lefranc's wine began to attract attention, including the likes of President Ulysses S. Grant, who traveled to Almaden for a visit and a tasting. Given Grant's well-known thirst for adult beverages, the event was probably more of a drinking than a tasting. Very special visitors might have been treated to equally special vintages from a secret wine cellar accessed through a trap door in Lefranc's dining room. Besides its wine, Almaden was known for ribald entertainment. One memorable soiree included stage actress Annie Held bathing in sparkling wine, a shocking display for the time.

Tragedy struck in 1887 when a case of wine fell off a wagon being driven by Lefranc himself. The crash spooked the horses, sending Lefranc tumbling under the wheels and causing his untimely death. His son, Henry, took control of the estate, but he too was killed in a freak accident. Direction of Almaden then fell to Lefranc's daughter, Louise, and husband, Paul Masson, yet another Frenchman who had been working at Almaden for several years. Masson directed the estate successfully, but the souring effects of Prohibition convinced him to trade Almaden to Charles M. Jones in 1930 for a 26,500-acre

ranch near Gilroy, California. Jones continued to make legal medicinal and sacramental wines until Prohibition was repealed, when he successfully returned the estate to commercial wine production until his death in 1940.

LOUIS BENOIST: LIVING THE DREAM

Wealthy San Francisco socialite Louis Benoist acquired control of the Almaden Vineyard in 1941. He was enamored with Napoleon Bonaparte's life to the extent that his home was decorated with various objects of art and memorabilia recalling the French monarch's reign. Thus, perhaps it was no surprise that Benoist set about replanting the vineyards, upgrading the cellars, and resurrecting the brand in a very aggressive manner. He hired top experts in both production and marketing, resulting in the introduction of "varietal wines." These were labeled by the name of the grape, such as Chardonnay and Pinot Noir, rather than continuing the old U.S. industry standard of borrowing geographical names from Europe, such as Chablis and Burgundy.

Such revolutionary packaging begged equally creative publicity and promotion. Benoist's campaigns included buying two airplanes to bring in wine media personalities, distributors, and retailers to see, hear, and taste Almaden's new virtues. Such visitors were royally entertained with exceptional fare created by highly acclaimed chef Louise Savin. No fewer than seven estate homes were outfitted with the best of comforts for these guests, who were also treated to a short cruise on Benoist's four-masted schooner, *Le Voyageur*. These odysseys became icons of Almaden entertaining, and decision-making market reps left the estate fully sold on the new varietal wines. Sales took off in much the same manner as the company's aircraft. By the mid-1960s, Almaden sales, led by the wildly successful blush wine Grenache Rosé, surpassed the million-case level each year.

Benoist foresaw industrialization moving into the Los Gatos area and the reality that Almaden's success would attract plenty of competition. He decided to sell the estate to the large National Distillers beverage company in 1967. That company eventually took the brand into the huge San Joaquin Valley for value-priced wine production. Today, the Almaden wine brand is managed by the Wine Group.

PAUL MASSON: NO WINE BEFORE ITS TIME

With wealth both earned and inherited, Paul Masson had the means to fulfill a vision of making fine sparkling wines. While directing Almaden Vineyards operations in Los Gatos, he constructed his own cellars in 1901 near the town of Saratoga. Four years later, Paul Masson California "Champagne" was held high in many toasts of health and prosperity at the newly constructed Masson Château. His wife, Louise Lefranc Masson, was, rather curiously, a Prohibitionist and would have none of it. Nevertheless, she was a gracious hostess, and an invitation for an evening at the Masson Château was lofty social recognition for both celebrities and the local gentry.

Thanks to national Prohibition, the Masson estate was sold in the early 1930s. Following repeal, the new ownership renamed the estate Mountain Vineyards, and the good times returned with a series of summer concerts for the public, although those were a far cry from the grand free-flowing bubbly wine soirees held there decades earlier.

Success burgeoned until once again succumbing to changing times. The surge of industrial development in the Saratoga area brought an insatiable demand for land. As real estate prices soared, and land tax rates along with them, growers and vintners had little choice but to cut and run. The Paul Masson name was acquired by the giant beverage company Seagram's, who made it a brand for wines produced in its huge San Joaquin Valley winery. They hired actor Orson Welles to launch the

famous advertising phrase "We will sell no wine before its time."

GEORGES DE LATOUR: FRENCH CONNECTION

By the time Georges de Latour arrived in California in 1882 from France, gold prospecting had become sparse. He founded a firm that purified potassium bitartrate (cream of tartar) from wineries; business was successful, and his company merged with the Stauffer Chemical Company in 1897. The following year he married Fernande Romer from Alameda, California.

On a quest for a Napa Valley winery, the couple found a vineyard that California State Senator Seneca Ewer had built in 1885 near the

❧ André Tchelistcheff: BV's Winemaking Giant ❧

DESPITE A physical stature that did not reach five feet in height, André Tchelistcheff was one of the tallest winemakers in terms of Napa Valley distinction. Born to a prominent family in Moscow in 1901, Tchelistcheff (pronounced "chellist-shef") was a White Army soldier serving in the Russian Civil War. Wounded by gunfire and left for dead in a snow-laden battlefield, he managed to survive and rejoin his family.

While studying agriculture in Czechoslovakia and then winemaking at both the Institut National Agronomique and the Institut Pasteur in France, he was introduced to Georges de Latour. In 1938, Latour offered Tchelistcheff the position of vice president and chief winemaker at the Beaulieu Vineyard. From the start, Tchelistcheff introduced French methods, which transformed not only Beaulieu Vineyard's procedures and techniques but those in all of Napa Valley. Despite being a chain smoker, he had a sharp palate, and that and his quick wit endeared him to his colleagues, who often called him "the maestro."

Perhaps his most publicly visible achievement was the development of the Beaulieu Vineyard Georges de Latour Private Reserve wine, which was the first of the now popular reserve editions of top-quality production featured by prestige vintners. It was also the first truly distinguished California Cabernet Sauvignon to compete favorably against Bordeaux imports. Some of the top vintners rising into California wine prominence worked for Tchelistcheff at BV one time or another.

California Wines
MADE FROM
CALIFORNIA FRUITS

charming hamlet of Rutherford. When Fernande first saw the estate in 1900 she exclaimed, *"Quel beau lieu"* (what a beautiful place). Shortly thereafter, the de Latours purchased the four-acre winery and founded the Beaulieu Vineyard brand.

Georges was instrumental in bringing to California some of the grafting techniques that were resurrecting European vineyards from the dread phylloxera root louse blight, but Prohibition was even quicker than phylloxera in shutting down wineries. Clever marketing of the Beaulieu Vineyard brand, known simply as "BV" by wine geeks, endured by supplying altar wines to Catholic and Episcopal churches across the country, along with medicinal wines to hospitals. It was a business that actually served to

expand production. By the time of repeal, BV was producing more than a million gallons of institutional wines annually.

After 1933, Georges returned to the general wine market, pursuing a quality that could rival wines being imported from his native France. Russian-born André Tchelistcheff, adept in advanced French winemaking techniques, helped elevate BV wines to excellence, setting the bar higher for all premium Napa Valley vintners.

THE GALLO BROTHERS: DOING IT BY THE BOOK

Ernest and Julio Gallo were born to immigrants from the Piedmont winegrowing region in northwestern Italy. Their expertise was in growing grapes, and their San Joaquin Valley California vineyards supplied fruit to home vintners across America, who could legally make up to two hundred gallons per year during Prohibition. After repeal in 1933 opened up new commercial wine opportunities, the Gallo brothers, with less than $6,000 in capital and winemaking know-how gleaned from the local library, decided to jump into the wine business.

Julio took responsibility for production, while older brother Ernest looked after marketing. Their first several vintages were made into bulk wines that were sold to other vintners

experiencing post-repeal shortages. The Gallos saw beyond this, however, and moved from bulk to bottled wines. Their products were simple, tasty,

and—most important—cheap. One of their early major successes was Thunderbird, a sweet fortified white wine that sold for sixty cents per bottle. It was heavily advertised on radio with a jingle that became wildly popular:

> *What's the word?*
> *Thunderbird!*
> *How's it sold?*
> *Good and cold!*
> *What's the jive?*
> *Bird's alive!*
> *What's the price?*
> *Thirty twice!*

Another of the Gallo winners was Ripple, one of the so-called pop wines of the 1970s. It had a low alcohol content and was the butt of frequent playful quips by late-night television talk show host Johnny Carson. Ripple became even more highly visible to the public as the chosen favorite of Fred Sanford, played by Redd Foxx in the hit TV series *Sanford and Son*.

Creating Dago Red

DURING THE 1920s and 1930s, Dago Red was almost synonymous with wine. It was the time of Prohibition, when the American economy was sliding into the abyss of depression. There was little work, especially for immigrants who could speak little or no English. Workers considered themselves fortunate to find any work, even jobs that lasted only a day or two. Italians were among the most skilled tradesmen and were eager to accept "one day and then go" jobs. Out of this came the rude tag of "day-go," shortened to *dago*, for Italian Americans.

Wine was, of course, a staple of Italian diets, and expensive bottled goods were out of the question in the tenement neighborhoods of big cities. Fortunately, the Volstead Act allowed heads of households to make up to two hundred gallons of wine each year, but only for family consumption. Growing grapes in the cities was, of course, not an option. But inexpensive grapes were available from California. Alicante Bouschet grapes were so dark and rich that a gallon of them crushed could be stretched to two with some added sugar and water. A few days of fermentation and presto-vino—Dago Red!

While it was cheap and ordinary, Dago Red ironically saved many prestige California vineyards from demise. Indeed, vineyard acreage actually increased during Prohibition. The Italian American brothers Ernest and Julio built the foundation of their Gallo wine empire by selling grapes to markets across America during that time.

Gallo wines were not, however, the choice of serious wine enthusiasts. But the Gallos knew there were many more people who could not afford serious wine than there were highbrows who could. The combined genius of the brothers paid off in monumental fashion, as they became the largest single vintner in the world and the largest privately held corporation in America.

Ernest and Julio Gallo? The two brothers who made it possible for man to fly.

—Johnny Carson, host of the *Tonight Show*

ROBERT MONDAVI: EMBATTLED VISIONARY

 In 1943 Cesare and Rosa Mondavi purchased the well-established Charles Krug Napa Valley winery. They were Italian immigrants who had had success in building a Lodi, California, fruit-packing business. Sons Robert and Peter were hard workers at their folks' winery but harbored a festering sibling rivalry.

Cesare died in 1959, leaving Rosa to run the business. When an invitation arrived for Robert and his wife, Marge, to attend a White House function in November 1965, the family discussion centered on the expense of the event. Robert argued for attending, citing the opportunity for good winery publicity. He and Marge had already drained their budget to buy her a fur coat to wear to

Washington. Peter objected to the foolish waste of money and even accused his older brother of taking company funds to pay for it. Then the fur really flew as Robert took some swings at Peter. Mama Rosa broke it up, firing Robert and setting off family fireworks that were heard around the wine world.

Without demure, a determined Robert Mondavi secured financing to build the first major post-Prohibition Napa Valley winery. The Robert Mondavi Winery emerged as an ultramodern facility decorated in Spanish mission-style that stood in stark contrast to the older valley wineries. Mondavi's vision was more than bricks and stainless steel. He was convinced that he could meet or beat the quality of the best the world had to offer by improving on traditional methods.

After returning from a trip to the European wine regions, Mondavi commenced to integrate some Old World techniques with state-of-the-art methods developed at the University of California at Davis. The idea was to make entirely new expressions and styles of California wine. One of his first releases was the now

⦿ Burying the Hatchet ⦿

IN 2005, Robert Mondavi and his brother, Peter, put their differences aside and made a symbolic barrel of red wine together they called Ancora Una Volta (together once again). Robert was inducted into the California Hall of Fame in December 2007 by Governor Arnold Schwarzenegger and then First Lady Maria Shriver. Robert Mondavi will be forever honored for the generous contributions he and his family made toward creating the Mondavi Center for winegrowing research and teaching; the center opened at the University of California at Davis in 2002.

famous Fumé Blanc, a white table wine made from Sauvignon Blanc grapes in the style of the Pouilly-Fumé district of the Loire Valley in France. Cold fermentation preserved the fruit-forward flavors, which were carefully matured in new French oak barrels. California-grown Sauvignon Blanc varietal wines had previously languished in the U.S. market, but the early 1970s release of the Robert Mondavi Fumé Blanc resurrected the grape to a stunning success. It was an astute winemaking innovation that launched the Robert

Mondavi Winery brand as one that set new standards for California wine.

LINDEMAN AND PENFOLD: VISIONARIES DOWN UNDER

Among the plethora of Australian wines now found in the world marketplace, there are two standout labels that continue from bold nineteenth-century Aussies: Lindeman and Penfold.

A native of Surrey, England, Dr. Henry John Lindeman was a Royal

Navy surgeon who had visited vineyards and wineries in both France and Germany before immigrating to New South Wales. He planted his first vines in 1843 along a Paterson River site and settled in as a winegrower of modest production. Lindeman quickly foresaw the commercial benefits of encouraging the New South Wales government to rescind the expensive license necessary for winegrowing so he could expand his output. The lower costs enticed small vintners to enter the business, resulting in a doubling of the region's vineyard acreage within the next decade.

In 1844, just one year after Lindeman planted his first vineyard, Dr. Christopher Rawson Penfold established a vineyard at his Magill estate on the foothills of the Adelaide Range. Penfold was an ardent believer and promoter of wine as

❧ Captain Cook's Cloudy Bay ❧

CLOUDY BAY Sauvignon Blanc took the wine world by storm in the late 1980s. The bold bouquet and flavor notes of grapefruit enhanced by complex herbal nuances moved the wine far beyond the shy flavors masked by the usual oak-barrel aging of white Sauvignons produced in French wineries. Other vintners soon followed, and New Zealand Sauvignon Blanc emerged as the global standard for this white wine varietal in the 1990s.

both a medicine and a therapeutic quaff. He produced the classic Port and Sherry types that had become traditional in Australia but was also one of the first to develop commercial quantities of table wines from German and Bordeaux vine varieties. Penfold became an ambitious commercial vintner, producing more than a hundred thousand gallons of wine in 1871, which was then about 15 percent of all wine grown in South Australia.

ROMEO BRAGATO'S PROSPECTS

Any enthusiasm that had existed for a Kiwi wine industry was dampened by the late-1880s discovery of the same phylloxera root louse that had destroyed most of the classic vineyards in Europe.

In 1895 Romeo Bragato, an Italian-born expert in viticulture, was invited to study New Zealand's troubled vineyards. Subsequently, he wrote a report to the host government titled *Prospects of Viticulture and Instructions for Planting and Pruning*, in which he encouraged replanting vineyards with resistant vines from America to

abate the phylloxera. Bragato also suggested forming viticultural districts in New Zealand that were best adapted to the soils and climates of specific vine varieties. Unfortunately, response by both government and winegrowers was minimal, and by 1900 the vineyards of the nation were fully infested with the root louse.

Bragato received a second invitation from the New Zealand government—this one an offer to take a permanent position as the first viticulturist and head of the Viticultural Division of the Department of Agriculture. He accepted and commenced work in 1902. In the next several years, he imported a selection of classic vine stocks and instructed winegrowers in the proper manner of grafting on disease-resistant rootstocks. He again made recommendations for which varieties should be planted where. Active response was yet again rather dispassionate, and in concert with Prohibition, the New Zealand wine industry languished for the next sixty years.

New Zealand's repeal came at the end of the 1960s. That, along with a growing consumer awareness of fine wine through easy travel to Europe and the much heralded success of Australian and Chilean wine

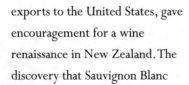

exports to the United States, gave encouragement for a wine renaissance in New Zealand. The discovery that Sauvignon Blanc could be grown to a quality unequaled even in France now has New Zealand firmly on the world wine map.

7

Fascinating Legacies

THE WORD *enophile* is the English-language corruption/combination of the Greek *oinos* and the French *phile*, which together mean "wine lover." Enophiles as well as everyone else can enjoy some bizarre events in the wine world

that make for some entertaining stories. Consider GI Joes and Janes returning home from World War II in the 1940s who told of a popular British drink that stretched expensive Champagne with cheap German wine and was garnished with a hard red cinnamon candy. The result was a ribald cocktail known as the One-Balled Dictator, a nod to the rumored anatomical deficiency of Adolf Hitler. A more recent popular tale is about the late great undersea explorer Jacques Cousteau, who found some sealed Greek wine amphorae in ships that had sunk

off the coast of Marseilles in the second century BCE. The obvious question was, Did he drink the wine? Cousteau supposedly answered, "It was delicious!" Such wine was, of course, far from drinkable—even for a Frenchman. This chapter opens up the history book to more such yarns.

MAKING THE DEVIL DO IT

Don Melchor de Santiago Concha y Toro inherited vineyards in Chile during the 1860s, but they produced wines that were easily forgettable. He hired a French winegrower to replant with Bordeaux vines, imported before any of the phylloxera root louse had infected them. The resulting wines were much better, and some brought the excitement that

Don Melchor had envisioned. Those that were particularly superior were placed in a special family reserve cellar to age further, but one might expect, bottles increasingly came up missing. Continued thievery prompted a local rumor that the devil lived in the reserve vault. Subsequently, a sign was placed over the entrance of the cellar signifying that it was the *Casillero del Diablo* (cellar of the devil). The idea was obviously designed to

frighten the looters away, and it worked perfectly—the thievery stopped. Indeed, the tale spread so far and wide that the Casillero del Diablo became a global phenomenon and is still one of the historic Concha y Toro wine estate's highly successful labels.

TH.J. OR NOT TH.J.? THAT IS THE QUESTION

Amid the December 5, 1985, listings at the esteemed Christie's London auction house was an exceptionally rare Château Lafite 1787. Hardy Rodenstock, a celebrated German wine collector, offered this remarkable old flagon as part of a cache of historic wines retrieved from an old building in Paris razed for a development project. This particular bottle was engraved with the initials "Th.J.," suggesting that it was once owned by Thomas Jefferson, the American minister to France from 1785 to 1789.

Christie's experts had reportedly carefully examined Rodenstock's bottle before accepting it for auction. It had all the size and shape expected of a Jefferson bottle, and bidders were assured in the catalog that this 1787 Lafite could "rightly be considered one of the world's greatest rarities." The auctioneer was world-famous wine expert Michael Broadbent, author of several authoritative reference books for old Bordeaux vintages. Nobody questioned the bottle  because Rodenstock was a figure frequently mentioned in the wine media for throwing lavish private tastings of his rare vintages for highbrow wine aficionados.

As bidding continued to accelerate, the audience gasped when Broadbent's gavel came down with an eye-popping winning bid of £105,000, about US$157,500! It was a new world

☙ *Fateful Etchings* ☙

IN PREPARATION for a 2005 exhibition at the Boston Museum of Fine Arts, experts questioned the authenticity of Bill Koch's four prized Jefferson 1780s bottles of Châteaux Lafite and Mouton. This skepticism was further endorsed by Thomas Jefferson Foundation officials and later confirmed by further sleuthing, which included bottle etchings made by an electric power tool. Koch was enraged and hired a team of investigators to track down Rodenstock and bring him to justice. The tracking down part has been accomplished, but at this writing the justice part remains.

record payout for a single bottle of wine. The successful bidder of the Th. J. Lafite 1787 was Kip Forbes, son of publisher Malcolm Forbes. As one might expect, the elder Forbes was as stunned as most everyone else in the wine world when he learned what his son had paid for their new family treasure.

The Forbes bottle served to create plenty of notoriety, which prompted other serious collectors to seek out Jefferson bottles. Billionaire Bill Koch, recognized globally as the owner of the yacht *America³*, winner of the 1992 America's Cup, bought four of Rodenstock's Jefferson bottles for $500,000 and proudly showed them off to friends privileged to visit his expansive cellar.

OOPS!

A very rare 1787 Château Margaux was taken on consignment for sale by William Sokolin, a well-known New York City wine merchant. With the late 1980s' escalating "can you top this?" auction prices, Sokolin listed the relic at $519,750. To publicize his treasure, he took it to the Four Seasons restaurant to show it off to deep-pocketed enophiles. During the festivities he managed to drop it, and of course, the old brittle bottle smashed on the floor. The broken pieces of the bottle brought an insurance settlement of $225,000. Ironically, the old Margaux that slipped out of Sokolin's hands may have also slipped Sokolin out of a legal mess had he succeeded in selling what may have been a bogus bottle. In any case, headlined stories of the event brought fame to him and valuable publicity to his business.

The oldest bottle of wine sold at auction was a 1646 vintage Hungarian Tokaji at Sotheby's in London in 1984 for about $1,000.

THE CHECK PLEASE!

Several fun-loving employees at Barclay's Bank went out on the town in 2001 to celebrate a successful business deal at the posh Petrus restaurant in London. They matched dinner with bottles of the highly coveted namesake Château

Petrus, vintages 1945, 1946, and 1947—some of the finest and most expensive Bordeaux. The check came to about $62,000! The gracious restaurateur did not include the cost of the food in the check, but still, *holy expense account!* They were, of course, fired.

I'd rather have a bottle in front of me than a frontal lobotomy!

—Tom Waits, singer-songwriter, on *Fernwood 2 Night*; also attributed to W. C. Fields

NAUGHTY LABELS

While American freedoms of the press are beyond liberal traditions, it's a different story when it comes to wine labels. The list of shall-not-contain items in the U.S. Code of Federal

Courtesy of Kenwood Vineyards

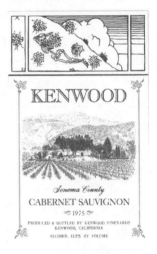

Courtesy of Kenwood Vineyards

Regulations, Section 27, includes a plethora of wine regulations that exceed most common

interest. One provision is found in Section 27, Part 4.64(3), which prohibits "Any statement, design, device or representation which is obscene or indecent."

Testing this statute was the 1975 vintage of Kenwood Vineyards' Artist Series Cabernet Sauvignon, with the now famous Naked Lady label. The label reproduced David Lance Goines's painting of a nude reclining in a meadow under a tree. Kenwood management was, of course, distressed by federal disapproval because the artwork was an expensive commission. Goines retaliated by repainting the same scene substituting a skeleton for the young woman. As any market-savvy person would expect, this story made for endless media grist and served to rapidly sell out the vintage. The few original 1975s that remain are expensive collector's items.

The Baroness Philippine de Rothschild of Bordeaux celebrated the 1993 vintage of her Château Mouton Rothschild with label artwork exhibiting a reclining nude pubescent girl drawn by French artist Balthus. It seemed rather vanilla—nothing obscene or indecent about it— certainly much less in anyone's face than what was readily available in the media. Nevertheless, the U.S. government nixed it, and the baroness reluctantly complied, leaving the space blank on labels of the 1993 Mouton destined for the U.S. market. The European wine media had a field day poking fun at America for such silliness.

JUICY WINE SCANDALS

There have been wine swindles in the marketplace since ancient times. The Roman Pliny the Elder was sure that with so much "fine wine" supplied to the aristocracy, a good share of it had to be counterfeit. On the darker side, Roman Empire vintners added lead to wine to make it taste sweeter, doubtlessly unaware that they were poisoning their customers. In 1985, some equally overzealous vintners in Austria were charged for using antifreeze (diethylene glycol) to sweeten their wines. That was a particularly bad year for poisoned wines; thirty Italians were hospitalized, and eight died from drinking some Piemonte wines laced with toxic methyl alcohol.

The French found many fraudulent wines emerging after the phylloxera root louse epidemic in the early 1900s. Crooks bottled cheap wines under prestige labels and blamed the "different" taste on the effect

of grafting on American roots. Out of this came the now familiar Appellation d'Origine Contrôlée (AOC) in 1935, which regulated documentation of wine provenance. That system has since been updated as the Appellation d'Origine Protégée (AOP).

Other European nations followed the original French AOC decree, but unscrupulous vintners and merchants still found ways to manipulate identities. One of the most famous cases was one involving Lionel Cruse in 1973. Cruse, as director of the then 155-year-old highly respected wine marketing firm Cruse & Fils Frères, was one of eighteen merchants charged with falsifying documents and labels. The press reported cheap red wine from the expansive Pays d'Oc region of southern France being brought to Bordeaux chateaux for stretching inventories of high-end classified wines. It was a time when the Watergate scandal was rocking the United States, and thinking that Richard Nixon was innocent, Cruse defended his plight by announcing, "You'll see, I'll be the Nixon of Bordeaux." He was, although much differently from what he had anticipated. His trial exposed his part via testimony from a wine broker and a tank truck driver who admitted to phantom blends of Bordeaux, which some called "Château Mystery."

Among other cases was the South African scandal of 2003, when essences of green pepper were added to some South African white Sauvignon wines to enhance the natural peppery character flavor profile. In response, the South African government posted new regulations requiring their Wine and Spirit Board to closely scrutinize varietal wine character before permitting wines to be released to the marketplace.

In 2005, the famous Beaujolais vintner Georges Duboeuf was charged with blending ordinary

wines with classified growths and marketing them at fine-wine prices. A trial found that his company had committed "fraud and attempted fraud concerning the origin and quality of wines."

French vintners struck yet again. Six bulk wine producers in southwest France were convicted of selling giant E. & J. Gallo of California more than three million gallons of fake Pinot Noir during a three-year period before 2008.

ROAMING GOATS: FUMING FRENCH

Charles Back first produced his Goats do Roam red in 1998 as a quirky way to telegraph that his red wine was similar to that grown in the Côtes du Rhône of southern France. The idea was also a play on the herd of Saanen goats that actually roam about on the Back estate in the Paarl locale of South Africa's West Cape Province.

The Goats do Roam blend was bottled under the Fairview Winery brand and exported to the United States. In 1999 the French government protested that Goats do Roam was an infringement on international trade names. As would be expected, the event caused a media stir that provided Charles Back considerable free market promotion and served to make the French look a bit fastidious. Success prompted Back to change the Fairview Winery name to the more recognizable Goats do Roam Winery, with an expanded line of Bored Doe and Goat-Roti labels that undoubtedly infuriate the French even more.

CATS IN THE BERRY BUSHES

Cynthia and Andrew Hendry founded their New Zealand Coopers Creek wine estate in 1980. Situated about thirty miles south of Auckland, in the Huapai and Kumeu wine districts, they planted about ten acres with Chardonnay and Merlot vines. Success encouraged the addition of a Sauvignon Blanc vineyard in the nearby Hawkes Bay region, an appellation then rapidly becoming famous for that variety.

Expert winemaker Kim Crawford was hired to wield his magic, bringing even more acclaim and demand for Coopers Creek wines. Conversely, the

1990s was a decade in which some insensitive wine writers referred to the most expressive styles of New Zealand white Sauvignon as smelling like cat urine. Some critics preferred to call it "sweaty." New Zealand's Lincoln University scientists identified it as a combination of fresh asparagus, snow peas, and gooseberries, and assured consumers that there was nothing to worry about. Whatever one chose to call such character, it was often intense.

Some of the vintners, however, did worry. It was a situation not isolated to New Zealand viticulture alone. California and even the vaunted Graves region of Bordeaux were often subject to negative quips from the media for bottling Sauvignon Blanc with a pungent character. Research scientists used high-performance liquid chromatography and other highly sensitive analytical techniques to identify ways to avoid the occasional nasty cat bouquet that had appeared in some vintages without warning. These studies have helped growers produce Sauvignon Blanc wines that are now revered as some of the most pleasant citrusy white wines grown anywhere.

Conversely, some vintners have identified a niche demand for the funky feline style and continue purposely producing it with whimsical wines. Coopers Creek actually flaunts it with their now famous Cat Pee on a Gooseberry Bush. Obviously they have a market, especially in

Britain, where it remains wildly popular.

THE SALAHIS: FUN AND GAMES IN THE WHITE HOUSE

A 1991 business and enology graduate of the University of California at Davis, Tareq Salahi returned to Hume, Virginia, to work with his family, founders of the Oasis Vineyard wine estate. A decade later he was tapped as a member of the Virginia Winery Board. He married King's College alumnus Michaele Holt in 2003.

It was an event that was graced by more than fifty bridesmaids and groomsmen, forty chefs, and an eight-foot-tall wedding cake.

On November 24, 2009, Tareq and Michaele crashed the White House to attend a state dinner. The media had a field day showing them being greeted by President Obama and enjoying the evening as if they were invited guests. Reportedly their escapade was to gather fame and celebrity so Michaele would be considered for the TV series *The Real Housewives of Washington D.C.* Whether or not their escapade was a crime or a prank, it paid off— Michaele got a part!

8

California Chronicles

SOME WINE ENTHUSIASTS trek to their favorite California estate wineries most every year with the eagerness reminiscent of the 1849 gold rush. Vintners welcome them, renewing personal friendships, and then it's off to barrel tastings of the new vintage with all the reverence of a baptism. Orders are taken, and bottle prices sometime reach what an entire case of the same wine might have cost just a decade or two ago.

Far-fetched? Maybe a bit, but California wines have achieved a quality that's been proven in head-to-head competitions to be the equal of or better than any of the premier wine regions in the world. A timeline drawn from Father Junípero Serra's 1770s mission vineyards along the El Camino Real to the present is linked with some charming, curious, and perhaps even surprising stories that have contributed to California's being perhaps the

most lauded winegrowing region outside of Europe.

CALIFORNIA: FROM WHENCE THE NAME

California is the name Colonial Mexico called its entire holdings in what is now the U.S. Southwest. For a land mass that large, it is curious that there is no definitive record of the origin of the name. Perhaps it was extracted from the Spanish *caliente fornalia* (hot furnace) or perhaps from the Native American words *kali forno* (high mountains).

Another possibility is that the word *California* appears in the fourteenth- to fifteenth-century mythical novel *Las Sergas de Esplandian* (Adventures of Esplandian), by Garci Rodriguez de Montalvo. In this story, California is a rocky Pacific island situated close to the mainland. It was ruled by Queen Califia, whose Amazonian-like women subjects worked their bountiful gold ore into tools and weapons. It was a tale sufficient to lure Conquistador Hernán Cortés on his 1536 expeditions to northwestern Mexico in search of this fantasy island and its cities paved in gold. Although he failed in finding the mystical land, Cortés did discover what is now called the Mexican Baja peninsula.

The Baja remains part of Mexico, but the *Alta* (upper), California, was part of a much larger territory that the United States acquired in the 1848

Mexican Cession Treaty for $15 million, a huge amount of money at the time. It turned out to be a bad deal for Mexico, however, when gold was discovered the following year; Cortés was obviously looking in the wrong place.

reached an enormous size, such as the Carpinteria vine in Santa Barbara County, which the U.S. Department of Agriculture reported had a trunk that measured nearly three feet in diameter and could bear several tons of grapes in a single vintage!

THE GIANT VINES OF SANTA BARBARA

Despite their thirst for wine, Mexican governors did little to encourage commercial winegrowing after the early 1800s El Camino Real mission trail was blazed in California by Padre Junípero Serra. It was a curious oversight, because for years the Franciscan monks had vineyards thriving where sufficient rainfall quenched the rich virgin soil. Some vines

NAPA: VIVID BEGINNINGS

Probably the most accepted version of the origin of the word *napa* is derived from the word *napo*, meaning "house" in the Patwin language of the native Wintun tribes who once lived in the Napa Valley. Other takes on the Patwin translation of *napa* are "fish,"

❦ Robert Louis Stevenson: Prelude to Napa Valley Prominence ❧

VISITORS ENTERING the Napa Valley see a welcoming billboard that quotes the tail end of a Robert Louis Stevenson phrase: "and the wine is bottled poetry." The passage from which these words are taken speaks to the virtues of Napa Valley wine but also salved the failures of gold prospectors, encouraging them to stay local and share a greater wealth in wine. Many did just that.

"grizzly bear," and "motherland." Whichever, the Wintuns were a colorful tribe whom settlers called "diggers" because they purged the flood plains of the valley's rivers and streams in search of edible grubs and worms. They were also hunters who wore animal skins in cooler weather and often donned no attire at all during the hot Napa summers.

■

So, bit by bit, they grope about for their Clos Vougeot and Lafite. Those lodes and pockets of earth,

more precious than the precious ores, that yield inimitable fragrance and soft fire; those virtuous Bonanzas, where the soil has sublimated under sun and stars to something finer, and the wine is bottled poetry.

—Robert Louis Stevenson, "The Valley"

SONOMA: THE LAST MISSION

Ask Sonoma locals what the word *sonoma* means, and they may tell you it's a Spanish word brought there by the early missionaries from Mexico. Padre José Altimira, for example, arrived in what is now the city of Sonoma during the 1820s to plan construction of the final mission on the El Camino Real trail.

But those in the know are aware that Altimira did not bring the word *sonoma* with him. Rather, it is more likely the Native American Chocuyen word for "Valley of the Moon," which Altimira selected for his settlement. There was a Native American Wappo tribe in the area known as Sotoyomes, whose name could have become corrupted to Sonoma. Yet another account is that Padre Mariano Payeras came to the area, even before Altimira, describing it as "the river of Petalumas and Sonoma."

SIERRA FOOTHILLS: GOLD IN THEM THAR VINEYARDS

The Spanish word *sierra* means "saw," a figure of speech used to describe the high, jagged sawtooth-like peaks of the Sierra Nevada mountains. The *nevada* (snow covered) mountains were a major destination of the 1849 gold rushers. It was a region that enticed many eager Europeans to California, each dreaming of

discovering the coveted mother lode and instant wealth.

Few, however, panned enough gold in the rapid streams even to fund their way back home. Instead of striking it rich, they were struck with fate and forced to settle where they were. Some of the prospectors had keen knowledge of Old World winegrowing and found themselves putting this expertise to work, making a living growing grapes or making wine. Thus, the Sierra Nevada foothills became one of the early centers of commercial winegrowing in California.

The Mission vines prevalent in the region made wines that surely brought little excitement to the European winegrowing hopefuls. The first Old World vines didn't arrive in Sonoma until the early 1860s and were initially planted in neighboring Napa as well. The lower valleys provided milder winters, better soils, and easier access to the San Francisco market. The California State Agricultural Society promised that "capital put into vineyards would bring greater returns than when outlayed in fluming rivers for golden treasures." Consequently, many of the failed European prospectors came down from the mountainsides to the promising valleys of Napa and Sonoma.

But some stayed in the rugged foothills, and Zinfandel evolved as one of the principal varieties to thrive there. The vineyards border streams that still attract dreamers panning for gold.

CALIFORNIA'S CENTRAL COAST: WINE ON SHAKY GROUND

William Palmtag was born to a German immigrant, a successful businessman who invested in a vineyard near San Juan Bautista in San Benito's Cienega Valley in the 1850s. Palmtag's good business sense did not, however, preclude him from unknowingly selecting his winery site on the San Andreas fault. Although Palmtag was unlucky, it goes beyond curiosity as to why Almaden Vineyards' management would decide to acquire that property in 1955 and erect the world's largest barrel-aging center there too! It was perhaps the same curious allure that drew the Derose family to buy the property in 1988. Adventuresome visitors who are welcomed at Derose Vineyards to taste and buy their wines can have a look at the winery floors, which shift a bit every so often.

PASO ROBLES: JESSE JAMES'S HIDEOUT

The city of Paso Robles centers the Central Coast region, a California winegrowing appellation that excels in vintages of prime Cabernet Sauvignon and other silky-smooth red wines. It is a locale that was also once the site of a hideout for Jesse James and his gang following a Kentucky bank robbery in 1868. Another very different retreat in the area was for world-renowned piano impresario Ignace Paderewski, who lived in Paso Robles while treating his arthritis in the local hot springs.

CARNEROS: PASTURE BECOMES TREASURE

An early Spanish land grant called the area along the north coast of San Francisco Bay "Los Carneros" (the sheep), a curious name, perhaps coming from the area's history as offering an idyllic vista of pastureland and farming. Mexican Governor General Vallejo parceled off tracts of the Carneros to buyers who planted vineyards as early as the 1830s.

But the area failed to develop in the aggressive manner of the Napa and Sonoma Valleys to the north, which had warmer climates.

Louis M. Martini, a respected Napa Valley winegrower, cited the Carneros as much better terroir for Pinot Noir vines than the warm climes inland. Subsequently, he ordered the first plantings of Pinots there in the 1950s, making vintages of red wines that increasingly attracted attention from the media and consumers. André Tchelistcheff, renowned Napa Valley winemaker at Beaulieu Vineyards, followed in 1972. Today, the old pastureland is revered as one of the prime California locales for Pinot Noir, Chardonnay, and other cool-climate varieties.

---ᘓᘓᘓ---

INFIDEL ZINFANDEL: MAKING WINE BLUSH

Neophyte enophiles question why otherwise perfectly sane vintners call a pink wine white. That, of course, is part of the novelty that first attracted consumer curiosity, along with the story of the wine itself.

By the 1970s, California vineyards were so profuse with Zinfandel vines that the supply of grapes from this particular variety had far outreached red wine demand. Zinfandel vineyards were being uprooted, and there was talk of more to follow.

A stuck fermentation of Napa Valley Zinfandel during the 1975 vintage season was discovered while Sutter Home production personnel were busy with the heavy workload of the vintage season. The problem was put aside, and later they found that only a small amount of red pigment had been extracted from the grape skins. The problem wine had a blushing pink tint, was sweet, and was packed with fresh

fruit flavor—far from the traditional red wine made from Zinfandel grapes. In a stroke of perhaps divine timing, the Sutter Home marketing folks learned of the wine and suggested pressing it out and restarting the fermentation as if they were making a white wine, although the finished product remained pink.

Sutter Home called it White Zinfandel, the first vintner to use the name for large commercial production, although the El Pinal Winery in Lodi, California, made a small amount of it in 1869. It was a pink wine that quickly became a popular novelty in a market thirsty for something different. Success, of course, resulted in other vintners jumping on the bandwagon, resulting in White Zin becoming third in national sales behind only Chardonnay and Cabernet Sauvignon during the 1980 and 1990 blush wine heydays. Some vintners made Merlot and other red grapes into pinkish wines, but none ever came close to the success of Zinfandel. At its peak of popularity, White Zinfandel outsold red Zinfandel more than five to one, and saved many Zinfandel vineyards from demise.

OPUS ONE: CONCEIVED IN BED

Translated from the Greek, *opus* means "creation." In the case of Opus One, it was the creation of an unlikely wine union of Château Mouton-Rothschild and the Robert Mondavi Winery. The idea was born in Hawaii during a 1970 meeting between Robert Mondavi and the colorful Baron Philippe de Rothschild, proprietor of the renowned Bordeaux wine estate. Not much came of that meeting until 1978,

when Mondavi visited Rothschild in France. The baron reportedly lounged on his bed while discussing business with Mondavi; later that day, the two great vintners agreed to embark on a joint winegrowing venture in Oakville, near the Robert Mondavi Winery.

It was a curious partnership because it was formed just two years after Napa Valley's rousing defeat of French wines in a major competition (heralded worldwide as the Judgment of Paris) and particularly so because the baron's own wine was one of the French losers. It was perhaps this event that motivated Rothschild to bring Bordeaux and Napa together to make vintages of an ultra-premium red wine from the classic native Bordeaux vine varieties grown in both locations.

The winemakers fermented the first Opus One vintage at the Robert Mondavi cellars in 1979. A case of twelve bottles was sold several years later at the annual

Napa Valley Wine Auction for $24,000, the largest amount ever paid for a California wine at that time.

Unfortunately, Rothschild died in 1988 at the age of eighty-six, a year before the contemporary-styled Opus One winery was completed. Mondavi survived for another twenty years. Their legacy of Opus One is perhaps the most celebrated label in the California wine industry.

MERITAGE: A NEW HERITAGE?

One of the progressive California winegrowing directions during the 1980s was the blending of typical Bordeaux grape varieties into higher-end wines that could attract customers from traditional French chateaux bottlings. Varietal wines are required to comprise at least 75 percent of the variety indicated on labels. Federal law prohibited U.S. winegrowers from calling any lesser blend California Bordeaux, despite archaic regulations that permit vintners to use California Burgundy and New York State Champagne, along with other obviously bogus appellations, as wine label descriptors.

Curiously, only a few of the great wine fathers have used the word *Claret*, a centuries-old British nom de guerre for Bordeaux red wines. That was a popular name for most any California red wine blend before Prohibition. Some newly adopted standards for Bordeaux-like production would seem to have made Claret a classic label readily recognized and accepted by Bordeaux lovers.

Instead, an association was founded in the late 1980s to come up with a new industry-regulated descriptor to reflect Bordeaux imagery. Thousands of names were submitted from across the United States and beyond. The winner was *Meritage*, pronounced like *heritage*. One can ask, Why not pronounce it with the French accent as well? In any case, decrees were drafted requiring all Meritage wines to be a superior product in a vintner's line, with a price point to match. Red Meritages were blends restricted, of course, to only the five traditional Bordeaux red vine varieties: Cabernet Sauvignon, Cabernet Franc, Malbec, Merlot, and Petit Verdot. Whites are similarly limited to Sauvignon Blanc, Semillon, and Muscadelle.

THE GREAT NAPA VALLEY TRAIN ROBBERY

The original Napa Valley Railroad was founded in 1864 by Samuel Brannan to provide economical travel for people and freight from San Francisco and Vallejo up the valley. Under Southern Pacific ownership, the rail line was extended south to Benicia in 1904, but in 1929, the line was limited to hauling freight, until it was shut down fifty-eight years later. Shortly thereafter, Vincent DeDomenico, president of the Rice-A-Roni food company, put together an investment group to buy the right-of-way to run a train for passengers to view the famous Napa Valley landscape while sipping the local wine and enjoying an onboard lunch or dinner. Old rolling stock, including a vintage coach that

was once part of the Ringling Bros. and Barnum & Bailey Circus train, were refurbished with elegant mahogany woodwork and plush fabrics.

The prospect of reopening a rail line through the middle of the Napa Valley didn't sit well with most residents and vintners because the diesel exhaust and noise promised to upset the serenity of the posh environs. Valley residents were already complaining that two-lane Route 29 was funneling too many tourists, tasting their way from Yountville to Calistoga. After considerable moral and legal confrontation, the DeDomenico group prevailed, and the first engine whistled its departure on September 16, 1989. Several daily shuttles ran from Napa city to St. Helena and back without incident, until

❧ *Truce in the Valleys* ❧

FOR THE Sonoma train robbers, the prank was all in good fun; but for many Napa Valley constituents, it was tantamount to starting a feud. The malice slowly diminished, returning to the usual somewhat friendly rivalry between the two famous wine valleys. In fact, in 2009, for the twentieth anniversary of the Napa Valley Wine Train, the Napa brethren conducted their own version of a hijacking. This time the train robbery brought attention to their esteemed annual wine auction. At last, it seems, the wine train may have found peace as one of the many attractions of the area.

one evening masked gunmen boarded the train from horseback and enacted a mock Wild West holdup. The group of onboard wine journalists were stunned into silence when their rolling dining experience was interrupted. The leader of the robbery spoof was

Jim Bundschu, of the respected Gundlach Bundschu wine families from the neighboring winegrowing area of Sonoma County. This clever stunt became the perfect opportunity for Bundschu and his Sonoma band to provide a tasting of *their* wines for the captives onboard. It worked out perfectly for the mock muggers, providing Sonoma County wine valuable publicity while also serving up a bit of embarrassment for their archrivals in wine, the Napa gentry.

CALIFORNIA VS. FRANCE: *BOTTLE SHOCK* IN PARIS

Most wine buffs have probably seen the movie *Bottle Shock*, a semicomedic account of Steven Spurrier's famous challenge that Napa Valley wines be judged against the finest from Burgundy and Bordeaux.

Spurrier was born to a wealthy English family. After learning the wine trade at Christopher and Company, London's oldest wine merchant, he moved to Paris and opened Les Caves de la Madeleine, a specialty shop featuring high-end French wines. Later, in 1973, he founded the first consumer wine school in France, L'Académie du Vin.

As part of a stunt quite obviously intended to dampen the American 1976 bicentennial celebration while also gaining some publicity, Spurrier organized a blind judging of California Chardonnay and Cabernet Sauvignon wines against an equal number of French white Burgundies and red Bordeaux. He was convinced that the growing reputation for California wine prowess would wane when confronted by the regal French classics.

As one would expect, the French wines were priced much higher than the California entries. The stacked deck went even deeper because all of the nine voting judges were French and included prestigious restaurateurs, media, governmental figures, and vintners. Each judge was

169

given the opportunity to award up to twenty points for each wine. Scores from the nine-member voting jury were then ranked.

In a surprise result that shocked Spurrier and, indeed, the entire wine world, Château Montelena Napa Valley Chardonnay 1973 and Stag's Leap Wine Cellars Napa Valley Cabernet Sauvignon 1973 were each decreed first place. One of the French judges was so upset she asked for her ballot back. The unlikely news was seen in the United States as supreme glory that could be relished by all non-French winegrowers.

❧ Continuing the Celebration ❧

FRANCOPHILE ADVOCATES quickly claimed that the French wine entries in the 1976 Judgment of Paris challenge were too young, and upon reaching maturity, would be preferred over the California wine competitors. This was actually put to the test with older Bordeaux and Burgundy wine entries at another similar tasting held in San Francisco two years later. California's Chalone won the Chardonnay competition, and Stag's Leap once again was the winning Cabernet entry. Even more contests have ensued, and California consistently takes top honors. The last of these was a thirtieth-anniversary Judgment of Paris tasting held simultaneously in London and Napa in 2006. California wines won yet again.

9

Charming Wine Characters

HISTORY IS BLESSED with people who have been very serious about wine and its many virtues—and its vagaries too. But wine has also been embraced by some winsome people since history's earliest times. Consider the words of Homer in his *Odyssey*:

> *Wine can of their wits the wise beguile,*
> *Make the sage frolic and the serious smile.*

These seem to be whimsical words from eighth-century BCE Greece, a time of instability among the nations' city-states. Fast-forward to Charles Dickens during the hard times of nineteenth-century England:

> *Fan the sinking flame of hilarity with the wine of friendship; and pass the rosy wine.*

Wine lovers who enjoy the lighter side of life should enjoy the stories of the interesting, articulate individuals you'll meet in this chapter.

CHAMBERTIN: BONAPARTE'S FAVORITE?

Napoleon Bonaparte is often said to have preferred red Burgundy from the coveted Chambertin vineyard, although there is plenty of evidence that the great French dictator selected Champagne as his wine of choice. His personal physician, Francesco Antommarchi, regularly prescribed Chambertin as part of the great general's regular diet, as well as a relief from both battlefield pains and political headaches. Perhaps this regal Burgundy was more the favorite of the good doctor.

When that this too solid flesh shall melt, and I am called before my Heavenly Father, I shall say to him Sir, I don't remember the name of the village, and I don't recall the name of the girl, but the wine was Chambertin.

—Joseph Hilaire Pierre René Belloc, speech at Saintsbury Club, Vintners' Hall (1912)

WINSTON CHURCHILL: BUBBLY PRIME MINISTER

The mention of Sir Winston Churchill among wine lovers can stir up a discussion of his love of fine Champagne and particularly that made in the Pol-Roger caves under the streets of Épernay.

Churchill was often publicly criticized for his frequent tipples of Champagne, a practice that had him at odds with London socialite Lady Astor. At one particular gathering, she informed him, "If you were my husband I would *poison* your coffee!" The statesman immediately replied, "If you were my wife I would *drink* it!"

Odette Pol-Roger was a member of the posh Belle Époque society of Paris and an unlikely courier for the French Resistance during World War II. She was a regal lady who found herself, unlike Lady Astor, captured by the charm and quick wit of the British prime minister, not to mention his publicly stated preference for her prestigious Champagne. He stated repeatedly, "I am easily satisfied with the very best." For him, the best was Pol-Roger 1928, which

was also favored by many others during the war years. Odette sent a case to him every year as a birthday present. In 1952, Sir Winston named his racehorse Pol-Roger and invited Odette to see the filly compete in England. The 1928 vintage ran out, but the annual birthday case was continued with the 1934 vintage, followed by the 1937, the 1945, and finally the 1947 until Churchill died in 1965. To express her sorrow, Odette ordered all Pol-Roger Champagne shipped to England to have labels bordered in mourning black; it was changed to dark blue in 1990 to honor Churchill's leadership in the British Admiralty. Churchill always regretted not having visited the Pol-Roger Champagne house but said it was "the world's most drinkable address." The house of Pol-Roger commemorated the

> ## ❧ *Savoring the Moment* ❧
>
> **SIR WINSTON** enjoyed both Champagne and brandy as much as his omnipresent cigars. One morning, after World War II was over, he arrived at his office at No. 10 Downing Street in London quite obviously under the weather from an evening filled with revelry. His secretary said something to the effect of: "Sir Winston, your consumption of strong drink since the war would fill your office up to here!" as she gestured to the chair rail. He looked up at the ceiling and said, "So much to do and so little time."

great statesmen with its first Grande Marque Champagne, Cuvée Winston Churchill—Vintage 1975, which was released at Blenheim Castle, Sir Winston's birthplace.

<hr/>

LEON ADAMS—GOTCHA!

One of the foremost wine writers in America was the late Leon Adams, who authored *The Wines of America*, an epic six-hundred-page history of American wine and winemakers. This and his other works were instrumental in wine education during the 1960s and 1970s. Adams lived in Sausalito, California, and loved wines from his home state, although he was not provincial and often wrote favorably about wines from other states and countries. He was a true professional enophile, quick to praise and promote any well-made wine.

One of many fascinating stories in his biography began with an invitation to speak at a national food and wine media luncheon in San Francisco, which he accepted with his usual humble grace. Arriving at the event, Adams was welcomed by some old friends and introduced to new writers, many of whom he sensed were Francophiles who hyped French wines out of social correctness. This was during the 1960s, when French wine was the in thing of highbrows across most of America, and the equally good, sometimes better, California wine was less popular.

Before the event, Adams selected two undisclosed white wines to be poured from covered wine bottles into the glasses heading each plate. One was a good California Chardonnay and the other, a fine white Burgundy also made from Chardonnay grapes. Before delivering his talk, he proposed a toast by raising the glass to the right, identifying it as the classic French wine, and encouraged everyone to compare it to the California wine, on the left.

Adam's speech was delivered with his typical eloquent and convincing style, as anyone would expect from this senior wine authority. To end his address, he asked his audience to take a taste from the glasses on the right again and for a show of hands from those who agreed that it was the superior of the two. The response was virtually unanimous. Adams stood quizzically silent for a moment and then offered a phony apology, saying that he had been mistaken and the wine on their right was actually the California Chardonnay. An awkward silence fell over the room. He had, of course, set them up, but it was

Adam's chance to make two important points to the righteous wine scribes: to trust their own palates, not current fashion, and write something about the California wine, which they had preferred over the French.

RODNEY STRONG: BALLET IN THE VINEYARDS

Rodney Strong came to California in 1959 as a retired ballet dancer, who had honed his taste for wine in France while performing on the Paris stage. He and his wife, Charlotte, his former dancing partner, set up shop in Tiburon, just over the Golden Gate Bridge from San Francisco. They bought bulk wines from other vintners, bottled them, and sold them under personalized wine labels, an innovation that became highly successful. They organized some investors and bought Windsor Vineyards in 1962. It was renamed Sonoma Vineyards and later became Rodney Strong Vineyards. Having been a World War II submariner, Strong had a periscope installed in his top-floor "bridge" office of the winery, a device he used to view the activities in his surrounding vineyards and, of course, to entertain the media and his marketing associates.

Sonoma County's recognition as one of California's finest wine appellations can be largely attributed to the character and vision of Rodney Strong. He was a pioneer in making and marketing wines from individual Sonoma vineyards instead of blending fruit from various sources. His single-vineyard labels attracted attention from the wine media and from his competitors, increasing the notoriety of the region.

Like his periscope, Strong had his ups and downs in business management. With advancing age, he lost control of his company, which was sold in 1989.

⸺⸺

WALTER TAYLOR: THEY DIDN'T GET HIS GOAT

A ribald spirit and free thinker, Walter Taylor was nevertheless a devoted wine purist. Two Taylor Wine Company uncles and several other management in-laws conspired to fire him for making denigrating remarks at a mid-1960s news conference about his family ameliorating wine with water to tone down acidity. At the time, the Taylor Wine Company in upstate New York was rapidly advancing to become one of the largest vintners in America.

Young Taylor cleaned out his office and promptly acquired the original site on which his grandfather had founded the family firm in the 1880s. The old winery, empty for decades, sat atop Bully Hill. "Bully for you if you can make it to the top!" was the subtle warning once given to those attempting to scale the steep hillside's rutted dirt road on the west side of Keuka Lake.

Without hesitation, Taylor labeled his wines as produced and bottled by the Walter Taylor Winery. When his family sold the giant Taylor Wine Company to Coca-Cola in 1977, legal demands were served upon Walter to cease and desist using the Taylor name in any manner. In colorful and clever response, he created new labels for his renamed Bully Hill Winery, with various line drawings of his face over which he painted raccoon-like eye masks. They created a stir that served to generate David vs. Goliath media stories, which actually worked to promote his new Bully Hill wine business.

Walter Taylor's next round of label art focused on a silly-looking goat that centered a public relations campaign playing on the plea, "They took my heritage and my name, but they didn't get my goat." Again, this served brilliantly to promote his Bully Hill Winery, with yet another round of free press coverage.

The Walter Taylor story has classic irony. The Taylor Wine Company no longer operates in Hammondsport, but the tiny Bully Hill renegade winery does and, in fact, has grown under the direction of Walter's widow, Lillian, to become the second largest in production volume among more than two hundred New York State wineries. A tragic automobile accident left Taylor a quadriplegic in the late 1980s, and he died a few years later. Bully Hill Winery thrives, attracting thousands of visitors, who now enjoy a smooth paved road all the way to the top.

I am certain that the good Lord never intended perfectly good grapes to be made into jelly.

—Fiorello LaGuardia, New York City mayor (1934–1945)

KONSTANTIN FRANK: VINIFERA WIZARD

Konstantin Frank's claim to fame was being the first viticulturist to succeed in commercially growing the regal Old World *Vitis vinifera* vines in the challenging cool-climate weather conditions inherent to New York's Finger Lakes winegrowing region.

Born and raised in Ukraine, Frank received a doctoral degree at the age of forty-two from the Odessa Agriculture Institute near the Black Sea in 1941. Curiously, he took his family out of the USSR during World War II into Nazi- and battle-ridden Austria. In 1951 the Franks emigrated to America, where Konstantin first found work as a janitor in a New York City restaurant and then as a

helping hand in the Cornell University experimental vineyards in Geneva, New York. Perhaps it was his brusque demeanor that landed him only menial work despite his advanced education in cool-climate viticulture back in Odessa. Dr. Frank's expertise was also overlooked by commercial vintners whose generations of forebears had failed in growing vinifera vines. On the other hand, Frank did not readily offer to share his expertise either.

In any case, one commercial vintner was keen on Frank's ability to grow Old World vines in the Finger Lakes region. It was Charles Fournier, president of Gold Seal Vineyards in Hammondsport, New York, who hired Dr. Frank as director of grape research. Fournier, once the winemaker at the famous Veuve Clicquot Champagne caves in

France, also had experience in cultivating Old World vines in cool-climate environs.

Frank planted select vine clones that had demonstrated good low-temperature endurance, then grafted them on rootstocks that suppressed excessive growth and trained them on regenerative trellis configurations. Several years later, thanks to Frank's methods, Gold Seal was able to release the first commercial New York State Chardonnay and Riesling wines.

Frank left Gold Seal in 1962 to found Vinifera Wine Cellars on his own vineyards, located on a beautiful plateau above Keuka Lake just north of Hammondsport. The serenity of his budding estate was in stark contrast to his caustic personality, which quelled the respect of his vintner peers. His success seemed to fuel a vendetta against the Finger Lakes wine industry, denouncing every grower of French hybrid vines by publicly exclaiming that they were growing grapes that made poison wines. Needless to say, he had few friends in the wine industry, but to his loyal followers in the marketplace, Dr. Konstantin Frank's fiery demeanor helped make him the eastern U.S. vinifera messiah.

JERRY MEAD: CRAFTY CURMUDGEON

Up until he died in 2000, at the age of sixty-one, Jerry Mead wrote the longest-running syndicated wine column in

America, "Mead on Wine." He had often remarked, "Any good wine will match well with any good food." Such stark 1980s and 1990s simplicity went totally against the grain of convention preached by highbrow foodie scribes. Jerry relished luring them into arguing against his one-size-fits-all wine premise. When good logic for the virtues of intricate flavor matching might seem to dispute his stance, he would revert to old saws like stranded-on-a-deserted-island scenes and "if all you had were a Cabernet and some fish . . ."

In reality, Mead loved matching good food with fine wine. His public voice for unfussiness was a standard around which he succeeded in bringing many neophyte wine drinkers to the true enjoyment of wine without getting caught up in any of the intimidating highbrow hype.

Jerry's wife, Linda, founded and published *W.I.N.O.* magazine, *Wine Investigation for Novices and Oenophiles*, in which Jerry's column "The Wine Curmudgeon" reigned as America's most vocal wine-industry critic. Few issues escaped his scathing editorials about how the Federal Bureau of Alcohol, Tobacco, and Firearms (the BATF, but now the TTB) or some state alcohol beverage commission had come down unjustly on the wine industry or how some wine marketer was exploiting unaware wine drinkers. Any sector of wine out of line could feel the sting of his wrath, particularly any journalists who preached wine and food fantasies.

His retirement to Nevada was thought by some to be a hideout from many angry souls who had felt the power of his pen, but thinking people revered and respected him. Anyone brave enough to confront him about his choice of choosing a Nevada retirement site, when little of his subscription and advertising income came from there, was quickly set straight. Typically, amid a few choice expletives, Jerry would cite the economic burdens of living in California and the wide-open culture of Nevada. Jerry Mead will forever be remembered as one of the most influential figures in creating

confidence among young New World wine enthusiasts.

■

As you get older, you shouldn't waste time drinking bad wine.

—Julia Child, food writer and television personality

FRANCIS FORD COPPOLA: HOLLYWOOD IN THE NAPA VALLEY

One of the familiar landmarks in the Napa Valley is the original Inglenook winery building constructed in 1879. The winery and vineyard estate was founded by Finnish sea captain Gustave Niebaum, who made a fortune in Alaskan fur trading. He was feared by cellar workers for frequent white-glove inspections

conducted to ensure shipshape sanitation. He died in 1908, and the winery was closed until the repeal of Prohibition.

Family survivors sold the property to Allied Grape Growers in 1964. The Heublein beverage company, the next owner, constructed a warehouse building directly in front of the historic winery facade. This was symbolic of the unfortunate events that had befallen once proud Inglenook.

Some of the estate's vineyards were sold to Hollywood film director Francis Ford Coppola in 1975. Twenty years later, he struck a deal for the winery buildings and remaining vineyards, but not the Inglenook name. Coppola set about renewing the winery in historic grandeur, renaming it the Rubicon Estate Winery, where all his wines are made. *Rubicon* means "no turning back" and perhaps refers to a grand commitment that would have surely pleased Gustave Niebaum.

❧ *Inglenook Returns* ❧

VISITORS ARRIVING at Rubicon are offered tours of the old Napa Valley cellars, including those that feature movie sets taken from some of the hit Francis Ford Coppola films. The Coppola touch continues restoring the property to its 1880 glory, such as removing the ugly storage building that Heublein management built in front of the estate in the 1960s. In 2011, Coppola acquired the Inglenook brand, returning it to the estate and Napa Valley prominence.

BACCHUS THE RASCAL

Jan Shrem grew up in Jerusalem with a passion for art. He was a child who liked to paint and draw, dreaming one day of being an architect. Failing math took architecture out of his future, but he found success as an encyclopedia salesman in college, earning enough to send money home to help support his family during World War II. This evolved to translating and publishing books in postwar Japan, where he found a taste for wine while courting his first employee, Mitsuko, whom he later married.

The publishing house became an empire that produced fabulous wealth and led the Shrems to the Napa Valley to fulfill their dream of a life of wine, art, and architecture. They selected a fifty-acre plot near Calistoga and commissioned the San Francisco Museum of Art to administer a contest among ninety-six accomplished architects to design "a temple to wine and art." Michael Graves won the nod, and construction of Clos Pegase was completed in 1987.

The winged horse logo was taken from a late 1800s painting by renowned French artist Redon and is one of many such fine art works displayed at the estate. One classic painting was delivered by a courier who guarded it personally in a first class airline seat from Europe. A luxury edition of Clos Pegase Cabernet Sauvignon was launched as the Hommage line; the label of each vintage paid homage to a different work of art.

Shrem opened his Cave Theater in the cellars of his winery to present *Bacchus the Rascal*, a media presentation that features some of the more colorful and risqué elements in wine-related art. He subsequently took the show on the road to share his precious wine-art collection.

◦ *Letting It All Hang Out* ◦

CLASSIC AMONG ribald wine labels was a Clos Pegase label designed with a colorful abstract painting by Jean Dubuffet that revealed an abstract male figure standing full monty. It was, as expected, quickly rejected by federal regulators. The Clos Pegase owner cleverly parlayed the event to gather attention from wine writers for his 1988 Homage series Cabernet Sauvignon release. The government required Shrem to, in effect, fully castrate and deflower the figure if he insisted on using the artwork for labeling, resulting, of course, in a second round of valuable publicity. Even more impressive was Shrem's years of persistent appeal to the federal government for a reversal that would restore the stark masculinity for a future label. A decade later, in a decision that both surprised and delighted free-thinking enophiles, the decree was reversed, allowing Shrem to use the original Dubuffet nude. Restored to his manhood, the figure reappeared on the 1998 vintage of the Clos Pegase Homage Cabernet Sauvignon. It was a decision that seemed to open the gates for all vintners to bring on Venus and David and every classical nude art form.

RANDALL GRAHM: BEGUILING VISIONARY

At the opposite pole of stodgy wine traditions is Randall Grahm's Bonny Doon Winery.

Grahm is an intellectual with an extraordinary ability to combine visionary research and experimentation into serious wines labeled with whimsical satire.

As a student at the University of California at Berkeley in the early 1970s, Grahm took a part-time job as a custodian in a wine retail store near his family home in Beverly Hills. Having the opportunity to taste all sorts of wines, from the worst to the best, he transferred to the University of California at Davis, where he earned a degree in plant science. After a stint with David Lett, a pioneer of Oregon's Pinot Noir repute, Grahm returned to California and planted a relatively modest vineyard near Santa Cruz, just south of San Francisco.

Among the vines planted were Syrah, Grenache, and Mourvedre—all classic Rhone Valley varietals. In 1984 he introduced the first wine packaged under his parody labels, the Le Cigare Volant. It poked fun at the winegrowers in the Châteauneuf-du-Pape district of the lower Rhone Valley who in 1954 had curiously passed a law forbidding the landing of flying saucers in their vineyards. The local French called them "flying cigars" and thus the label Le Cigare Volant. Another new wine followed that was labeled Old Telegram, a lampoon

◈ Last Rites for an Old Stinker ◈

RANDALL GRAHM'S concern for the environment is perhaps the most expressive among the world's vintners. In 2002, he held a Funeral for the Cork among friends and associates in New York City, complete with a hearse delivering a casket with the body of Monsieur Bouchon (Mr. Cork). Grahm delivered a eulogy for "the old stinker," a wake that celebrated his vision of the end of wines ruined by corks tainted by the formation of 2,4,6-trichloro-anisole (TCA), which has a distinct foul-mushroom odor.

directed at the classic Vieux Télégraphe vineyard, which is also situated in the Châteauneuf-du-Pape district. Yet another was his irreverent Cardinal Zin. These playful labels and the tasty wine behind them gathered considerable publicity; *Wine Spectator* magazine dubbed Grahm "the Rhone Ranger."

ED KING: THE LITTLE VINEYARD THAT COULD

Ed King III had every chance to pursue a top management career in King Radio, a large avionics firm that his father had founded and managed into a major company. Instead, young King was drawn to making forest products and started acquiring stands of timber in Oregon. One of these came with a small planting of Chardonnay, Pinot Gris, and Pinot Noir. Rather than pulling them up to make room for more Douglas fir

seedlings, father and son decided to see what kind of wine their little bonus vineyard would make.

The wine was good—actually very good. The Kings decided to expand the little vineyard and then again, and yet again. It proved to be an ideal locale for growing cool-climate varietals, and the little forest plot of vines grew to become 465 acres of vineyards and the single largest certified organic vineyard in the world. In 1991, the Kings completed construction of a full-fledged chateau winery south of Eugene, near the town of Lorane, a domain that would have fit perfectly on the golden slopes of Burgundy. With prime grapes and expert winemaking talent, the success for the King Estate was inevitable.

FRED FRANZIA AND TWO BUCK CHUCK: TAKING ON THE ESTABLISHMENT

Franzia brothers Joseph, Fred, and John formed the J F J Bronco Winery in 1973. For the first few years, the firm built a lucrative business, making and marketing bulk blending wines for other wineries, much like what their uncles, Ernest and Julio Gallo, had done in the 1930s.

J F J Bronco president Fred Franzia, again in Gallo fashion, moved forward from bulk to

bottled wines. Starting with the Forest Glen label in the early 1990s, he continued both buying and creating a few dozen other brands, such as Estrella and Domaine Laurier, which grew to wide distribution.

Among the most controversial of Franzia's acquisitions was the Napa Ridge brand name in a deal that stirred the ire of some of the upper-crust Napa Valley vintners. His value wine economics threatened the Napa upscale image, so a Napa consortium suit was filed citing that the wine Franzia bottled under the Napa Ridge label was neither grown nor bottled in the Napa Valley. It was a battle won but a war lost because Franzia responded by building a huge new winery at the southern end of the Napa Valley, which broadcast his presence and allowed J F J Bronco to buy Napa grapes and bottle wines under the newly legalized Napa Ridge label.

Along the way, Franzia also purchased the rights to the

◈ The Revenge of Two Buck Chuck ◈

J F J Bronco became a collection of brands and vineyards (California's largest vineyard owner) that created sales revenue in the hundreds of millions, all engineered from corporate headquarters housed in an unlikely complex of four construction-site trailers. Franzia saw his company as the champion of good wine for low prices and proclaimed that vintners pricing anything higher than $10 per bottle were, in his words, "greedy bastards."

Perhaps an even greater insult came when Two Buck Chuck wines started winning coveted awards: the 2002 Charles Shaw Shiraz garnered Best of Show honors at the Twenty-Eighth Annual International Eastern Wine Competition.

Charles Shaw Winery name, a once premier Napa Valley vintner that had folded. After one exceptionally productive vintage harvest from the huge Bronco vineyard empire, Franzia decided to package the bounty under the Charles Shaw brand over a simple California appellation. It was launched as a loss leader at Trader Joe's stores, and thus the wildly popular Two Buck Chuck was born, selling for two dollars and change. The use of a prestigious Napa Valley name, Charles Shaw, on the cheapest wine to be distributed across the entire country was, of course, another blow to the valley elite—and a retribution that continues their scorn.

JOHN KENT COOKE: FULFILLING JEFFERSON'S DREAM

Courtesy of Boxwood Estate Winery

John Kent Cooke was co-owner and president of the National Football League's Washington Redskins in the 1980s and 1990s. When his father, Jack Kent Cooke, died, the franchise went into a bidding war, which John lost by a few million dollars. Subsequently, Cooke and his wife, Rita, purchased the Boxwood mansion in the rolling landscape west of the Bull Run Mountains in northern Virginia. It was once the home of General Billy Mitchell of World War I fame. Mitchell was at the center of a famous court-martial trial for accusing the army and navy of incompetence for their slowness in building up air power. A guilty verdict ended his career but gained the publicity that proved the viability of military air power.

With the business of professional football in the past, the Cookes embarked on growing wine from Cabernet Sauvignon, Merlot, Cabernet Franc, and Petit Verdot vines grown in the style of the French chateaux that had

fascinated Jefferson more than two hundred years earlier. Their vision was to select a prime spot on their large estate, which sits squarely amid prominent country manors. Top consultants and designers were hired to establish a vineyard with clone-appropriate vines and to design a no-holds-barred winery that inspired award-winning architecture.

The result is an eighteen-acre estate of manicured vineyards supplying a stunning winery that operates with computerized precision. The Cookes employ a professional consultant, who makes frequent trips from Bordeaux to advise in the realization of their

exceptional Boxwood and Topiary blends, which are principally Cabernet Sauvignon and Cabernet Franc, respectively. Surely Thomas Jefferson would have been very proud.

We could in the United States make as great a variety of wines as are made in Europe, not exactly of the same kinds, but doubtless as good.

—Thomas Jefferson

10

Wine and Love

A LEGENDARY TAKE ON the discovery of wine is a Persian myth in which a harem girl was banished by a noble for lackluster performance. For this shortcoming, she was to drink fermented grapes, curiously then thought to be a deadly poison. After several tasty sips she became aroused and very much back in action. The king was, of course, pleasantly taken aback with the effect of the poison grapes on his paramour. Subsequently, he ordered all his vineyards a royal preserve. A charming story; however, there is considerable evidence that the sultry vixen's discovery was preceded by the clever Armenians.

While modern pharmacology is a boon to sexual performance, wine still seems to have a key role in stimulating both the idea of loving and the joy of lovemaking.

Clinical sexologists relate to the allure of wine's color—the red of passion caressed in a shapely wineglass. The integration of wine, love, and sex creates a wonderfully complex web that eludes complete understanding, but stories, poems, and songs continue to express the magic of savoring fine wine by amorous partners. This chapter takes us into their boudoirs.

rather Cinderella-like story, the youngest daughter is driven to labor long and hard hours among the vines. Solomon comes to visit his vineyard dressed as a commoner and sees the girl working in the vines, who is embarrassed by her unkempt appearance. The incognito monarch is taken with her and expresses his devotion in verses 7:8–9:

A LOVE SONG

Among the most sensuous of books in the Old Testament is the Song of Solomon. It has only eight chapters, and the setting is in King Solomon's vineyard, located about fifty miles north of Jerusalem. He had assigned its management to a mother and her two sons and two daughters. In a

> Now also thy breasts shall be clusters
>   of the vine. . . .
> . . . and the roof of thy mouth like the
>   best wine.

Knowing that Solomon had hundreds of wives, one has to wonder why he would have come looking for another or even a concubine. Thus, the tale is given to abstract interpretation, perhaps the most common being that the

Song of Solomon is a parable for the love of God for His earth.

RECIPES FOR LOVE

Most romantics are well aware that aphrodisiacs are love potions named for Aphrodite, the Greek goddess of love. Among the many ancient recipes to enhance male libido was pomegranates and oysters in wine, very popular among randy seniors looking for help expressing their affection. Some geezers still believe in such oyster function. In the third-century BCE Rome, Cato the Elder praised an elixir of wine mixed with berries from the myrtle tree, which was sacred to Venus, the Roman love deity. Pliny the Elder advised that the Egyptian wine Echolada was an effective stimulant for sensual pleasure. Ovid, a poet during Emperor Claudius's time, remarked, "Wine gives courage and makes men more apt for passion."

A CUP OF CHAMPAGNE?

According to the Greek legend, Helen of Troy was married to Menelaus, who had her sensuous breasts cast in wax. Helen also had "the face that launched a thousand ships," ships sent by Menelaus to Troy, where she was with her lover, Paris. The ships landed, and the Trojan War began; later, the now-famous huge

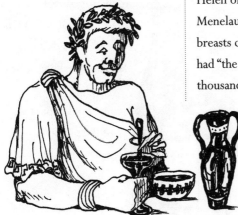

wooden horse filled with Greek soldiers entered the gates of Troy. Perhaps this tale prompted beautiful mistress Diane de Poitier to have wineglasses made in the shape of her bust as a gift to sixteenth-century King Henry II. Not to be outdone was King Louis XV's concubine Madame du Pompadour, who commissioned *coupe* glasses fashioned in the shape of her breasts. The Pompadour coupe was designed solely for Champagne, the trendy new wine of the courtiers in eighteenth-century France.

For French queen Marie Antoinette, the modeling of her petite left bosom was a matter of pursuing sensual pleasures of her own. She lavishly had dozens of glasses made in the shape for admirers to toast her health, her wealth, and perhaps her figure too with Champagne. The original mold was said to have been displayed in a Paris museum but has since been stolen. Fashion designer Karl Lagerfeld crafted a Champagne glass reportedly as a true likeness of actress Claudia Schiffer's left breast for the 2009 television biography of Marie Antoinette.

The breast-shaped coupe fell out of fashion after World War II in favor of the long sausage-shaped flute. Nobody has yet claimed responsibility for modeling that. Perhaps science can take credit, as glassmakers discovered that such a tall erect profile aids in keeping sparkling wines chilled, along with improved expression of the precious spiraling strings of bubbles.

CLEOPATRA'S CHARM

More than twelve hundred years after Tutankhamun's rule, Cleopatra VII shared the throne with her brother Ptolemy XIV, who was reputed to also be her husband. It was the first century BCE, and both were ambitious to be sole monarch of Egypt.

She drank and bathed in the finest wines—both perhaps to excess. Wine also served to enhance the allure and charms she advanced on Julius Caesar, whom she sought to enlist in bringing down her brother via a merger of Rome and Egypt. It was a scandal that was at the root of Caesar's assassination and left Egypt vulnerable to a Roman invasion. With her plot dashed, Cleopatra sailed off to Tarsus on her royal barge to seek an alliance with General Mark Antony. The meeting was a sensual event designed to enchant Antony with scantily clad maidens and, of course, plenty of fine wine. Cleopatra's seductive guile was more than the general could resist, and he was soon on board her royal barge, headed back to Alexandria. Outrage sprung up in Rome, and an armada was sent out to do them in.

■

Always do sober what you said you'd do drunk. That will teach you to keep your mouth shut.

—Ernest Hemingway

SPICY TURN-ON

A recipe called Hippocras was particularly popular in Europe during medieval times. It may have originated as an Asian love potion that evolved as red wine laced with cinnamon, cloves, ginger, sugar, and vanilla. The name is derived from filtering the mixture through a cloth much like that which the famous Greek physician, Hippocrates, used to strain herbs and spices from his wine medicines.

THE YELLOW ROSE OF TEXAS

Emily West traveled from New York to North Washington, Texas, in December 1835 as a fetching young woman serving in the household of wealthy rancher Colonel James Morgan. Several months later, while Morgan was leading his troops in battle against the Mexicans near Galveston, Mexican General Santa Anna halted his army to make camp on the ranch.

Santa Anna's plan was to continue in hot pursuit of Sam Houston's army the next morning, but most accounts tell of Emily having caught the general's eye. She was a beautiful young woman born of mixed-race parentage, then frequently referred to as "high yellow" in some circles.

Emily served the general an extensive Champagne breakfast that is thought to have

beguiled him and clouded his senses into a drunken stupor. Another version of the story insists that she was forced into the general's tent to serve his pleasure. Whichever, Santa Anna's reveling in the wake of Emily's charms and Champagne hospitality allowed her time to dispatch a ranch servant to alert Houston of Santa Anna's weakened condition. On April 21, Sam Houston maneuvered to defeat Santa Anna at the Battle of San Jacinto near what is now the city of Houston. Emily thus became the intrepid Yellow Rose of Texas, and April 21 is celebrated each year by patriotic Texans.

I have two words for you: Champagne.

—Pamela Anderson

WINE, WOMEN, AND SONG

The famous triad of sensual celebration and pleasure—wine, women, and song—was beautifully expressed in a waltz created by Johann Strauss in 1869. Curiously, the origin of the phrase is sometimes attributed to the devout cleric Martin Luther, who is quoted, "Who does not love wine, women and song remains a fool his whole life long." There is, however, a variation of this sentiment existing in German prose by Johann Heinrich Voss that predates Luther's time. In any case, this suggestive sybaritic idiom grew to become popular in ribald expressions embraced by cultures from Scandinavia south into Europe, east to Asia, and west to the New World. It was more recently corrupted to reflect far different mores in the punk rock song "Sex and Drugs and Rock & Roll" by Ian Dury and the

Blockheads in 1977—and followed by another version by the hard rock group Guns n' Roses.

WINE AND DATING

How brilliant is it that Olivier Magny created O Chateau? No, it's not a posh French vineyard estate but a clever concept of structured wine gatherings conducted on the Rue de la Folie-Méricourt in Paris. Eager singles lash out serious euros for Olivier and his sommeliers to wax eloquently while offering tastes of alluring wines. Games are played in which winners are awarded glasses of Champagne that can be shared with the person of their choice. Monsieur Magny says that O Chateau is a place of romance and that wine "helps with meeting people; it makes people more spontaneous, takes away inhibition." Indeed, his business may be the quintessential expression of *vive la différence*.

In 2008, Magny took his concept to cruises on the Seine and more recently has expanded to London under a different concept of matchmaking. Tables of six people, typically three ladies and three gentlemen, are entertained with wine, but before the second wine is introduced, the gents move to another table. It's the same with the third, fourth, fifth, and six wines. A gal can have a look at eighteen guys all while getting in the mood.

WINE AND SPICE

Dietitian Tanya Zuckerbrot regards a glass of red wine or Champagne as a good prelude to making love because it helps keep arteries open for the blood flow necessary for good sexual performance. Wine and sex is a time-honored combination, but how about wine *with* sex? Most every enthusiast of both wine and sex might admit to having thought about spicing up love organs with a splash of either a sweet white, a tasty red, or a bubbly sparkle. The thrill awaiting willing senses may be difficult to argue, but can mixing such flavors amid passion also help in achieving safe sex too? Wine contains ethyl alcohol, a well-known disinfectant, but is it sufficient to prevent infection from sexually transmitted diseases? Dr. Robert Frascino, who established an AIDS foundation, is quoted as saying, "No, unfortunately not. Wouldn't it be fabulous if it did?"

Other good doctors agree that wine poured on sex organs can irritate tender tissues, and the sugar and other organic compounds in wine can help promote infectious microorganisms.

BETTER THAN SEX?

Blogger Tamara Belgard relates that after a sumptuous dinner of fine wine and food, she listed the top ten reasons why the food and wine experience is better than sex:

- Condoms aren't required to eat or drink and there's never a risk of pregnancy.

- It's legal to pay for food and wine.

- Dropping $100 on a meal is perfectly acceptable.

- You can take pleasure from both food and wine in public and even in front of your family.

- You don't have to be committed to just one; feel free to eat and drink around.

- Food and wine won't leave you dripping with sweat or give you bed head.

- You can make dinner and a bottle last for hours, even all night.

- There's no obligation or expectations after you've enjoyed wine or food.

- You don't need mirrors, angles or toys to make the experience better.

- Sorry men, I love you all, but it just has to be said; women have a better chance of being truly and deeply satisfied by a good meal and a few glasses of fine wine.

WINE, WOMEN, AND CHOCOLATE

A good Pinot or bubbly before bed sounds enticing, but could it be that some ladies would rather have chocolate than sex? In a British study, a third of the women said they dreamed about chocolate daily, while only about half that many had sex on their minds.

Indeed, chocolate contains tryptophan and phenylethylamine, both precursors of complex compounds linked to passion.

But, sadly, research indicates that chocolate fails to deliver any amount significant enough to get a gal turned on. Any perceived effects are thought to be psychological because chocolate can stimulate energy and stamina for older gals—and guys too.

THE FEMALE SEXUAL FUNCTION INDEX

Vino e il sesso (wine and sex), a sensual subject in any language. Vino has brought *assatanto* arousal to women long before Rome made its empire. And who more than the Italians have brought wine and sex into every mode of *la dolce vita*? Every country can

argue the point, but it's Italy's University of Florence that conducted a study among eight hundred women eighteen to fifty years of age and found that wine does indeed prime female horniness. After one or two glasses of wine each day, they were assessed by physicians on the Female Sexual Function Index for measuring desire, pleasure/pain, orgasm, and gratification on a 36-point scale. The two-glass ladies scored an average of 27.3, the one-a-day women scored 25.9, and non-imbibers scored 24.4. One has to wonder what kind of roll in the hay earns a 36?

A woman drove me to drink and I never even had the courtesy to thank her.

—W. C. Fields, in *Never Give a Sucker an Even Break* (1941)

WINE AND DEVOTION

Are cultures that have a tradition of wine drinking more apt to have faithful marriages? Yes, say Jo Swinnen and Mara Squicciarini, researchers at the University of Leuven in Belgium. Support for this view was published in a working paper titled "Women or Wine? Monogamy and Alcohol," released in the December 2010 issue of the *Journal of the American Association of Wine Economists*.

Their work is based on centuries of data. Greeks and Romans were major winegrowers, and as their cultures moved forward, so did monogamy. Polygamous cultures, which featured concubines, harems, and monarchs with many wives, diminished. As Western civilization developed into Europe, the idea of monogamy became the accepted social morality. The authors also cite the rise of Christianity as a major influence for wine drinking and fidelity in marriage. Hundreds of medieval monasteries and nunneries grew wine. Mass and Eucharist celebrations symbolized wine as Christ's blood and condemned adultery as a mortal sin. Further, the advance of the Industrial Revolution provided wages for those who could not previously afford both drinking and supporting a family.

Swinnen and Squicciarini report that there is no compelling evidence for wine tippling leading to marital commitment but that their work reveals "a spurious correlation" of long-term social and economic factors that have led to ethnic monogamy associated with wine lifestyles.

Drinking wine is the second-most fun one can have without laughing.

—Unknown

Adams, L. *The Wines of America*, 3rd ed. New York: McGraw-Hill, 1985.

Alexander, P., ed. *The Lion Encyclopedia of the Bible*. Rev. ed. Herts, UK: Lion Publishing, 1987.

Butler, F. *Wine and the Wine Lands of the World*. New York: Brentano's, 1927.

Emerson, E. *Beverages, Past and Present*. New York: Putnam's Sons, 1908.

Evans, W., III, and A. Frothingham. *Crisp Toasts*. New York: St. Martin's Press, 1992.

Fiduccia, K. *The Quotable Wine Lover*. New York: Lyons Press, 2000.

Guhl, E., and W. Kohner. *The Greeks Life and Customs*. Old Saybrook, CT: Konecky & Konecky, 2009.

———. *The Romans Life and Customs*. Old Saybrook, CT: Konecky & Konecky, 2009.

Hailman, J. *Thomas Jefferson on Wine*. Jackson: University Press of Mississippi, 2006.

Johnson, H. *Modern Encyclopedia of Wine*. 4th ed. New York: Simon & Schuster, New York, 1998.

Kamp, D., and L. Lynch. *The Wine Snob's Dictionary*. New York: Broadway Books, 2008.

Kladstrup, D., and K. Kladstrup. *Champagne*. New York: Harper Perennial, 2005.

————. *Wine & War*. New York: Broadway, 2001.

Korach, M. *Common Phrases*. Guilford, CT: Lyons Press, 2001.

McGovern, P. *Ancient Wine*. Princeton, NJ: Princeton University Press, 2003.

Rosen, M., F. Jerome, and P. Harris. *Wine and Wisdom*. London: Think Publishing, 2005.

Standage, T. *A History of the World in 6 Glasses*. New York: Walker & Company, 2003.

Vine, R. *Wine Appreciation*. 2nd ed. New York: Wiley, 2007.

Younger, W. *Gods, Men, and Wine*. Cleveland, OH: World Publishing, 1966.

BORN AND RAISED in the Finger Lakes region of upstate New York, teenager **Richard Vine** worked with his grandfather making vineyard trellis posts. After a hitch in the U.S. Navy, Vine returned home in 1958 and began his winemaking career at the Pleasant Valley Wine Company (Great Western) in Hammondsport. While first a cellar worker and then a laboratory technician, he spent evenings earning a science degree at nearby Corning Community College.

In 1965, Vine was promoted to winemaker and assumed responsibility for more than six million bottles of annual wine production. In 1973, he became vice president of production at Warner Vineyards in Michigan. Four years later he accepted a research position at Mississippi State University, where he earned his baccalaureate and doctorate degrees while also writing the first of four academic wine books.

Purdue University gave Dr. Vine the call in 1991 to fill their initial Professor of Enology position. In 1999, Purdue dedicated a wine library in his name at the Nelson Food Science Building. During his university tenures, he served as the wine consultant for American Airlines

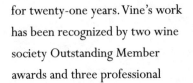

for twenty-one years. Vine's work has been recognized by two wine society Outstanding Member awards and three professional international knighthoods. Now retired, he writes wine columns for two periodicals.